THE COMPLETE GUIDE TO

Building Backyard Ponds, Fountains, and Waterfalls
for *Homeowners*

EVERYTHING YOU NEED TO KNOW EXPLAINED SIMPLY

by Melissa Samaroo

The Complete Guide to Building Backyard Ponds, Fountains, and Waterfalls for Homeowners: Everything You Need to Know Explained Simply

Library of Congress Cataloging-in-Publication Data

Samaroo, Melissa, 1982-
  The complete guide to building backyard ponds, fountains, and waterfalls for homeowners : everything you need to know explained simply / by Melissa Samaroo.
       p. cm.
Includes bibliographical references and index.
ISBN-13: 978-1-60138-598-7 (alk. paper)
ISBN-10: 1-60138-598-6 (alk. paper)
1. Water in landscape architecture. 2. Ponds. 3. Fountains. 4. Waterfalls. I. Title.
SB475.8.S26 2012
719--dc23

                              2011037465

Printed in the United States

PROJECT MANAGER: Gretchen Pressley • gpressley@atlantic-pub.com
BOOK PRODUCTION DESIGN: T.L. Price • design@tlpricefreelance.com
PROOFREADER: Sarah Wilson • sarah.alisha.wilson@gmail.com
FRONT COVER DESIGN: Meg Buchner • megadesn@mchsi.com
BACK COVER DESIGN: Jackie Miller • millerjackiej@gmail.com

Printed on Recycled Paper

A few years back we lost our beloved pet dog Bear, who was not only our best and dearest friend but also the "Vice President of Sunshine" here at Atlantic Publishing. He did not receive a salary but worked tirelessly 24 hours a day to please his parents.

Bear was a rescue dog who turned around and showered myself, my wife, Sherri, his grandparents Jean, Bob, and Nancy, and every person and animal he met (well, maybe not rabbits) with friendship and love. He made a lot of people smile every day.

We wanted you to know a portion of the profits of this book will be donated in Bear's memory to local animal shelters, parks, conservation organizations, and other individuals and nonprofit organizations in need of assistance.

– *Douglas & Sherri Brown*

PS: We have since adopted two more rescue dogs: first Scout, and the following year, Ginger. They were both mixed golden retrievers who needed a home.

Want to help animals and the world? Here are a dozen easy suggestions you and your family can implement today:

- *Adopt and rescue a pet from a local shelter.*
- *Support local and no-kill animal shelters.*
- *Plant a tree to honor someone you love.*
- *Be a developer — put up some birdhouses.*
- *Buy live, potted Christmas trees and replant them.*
- *Make sure you spend time with your animals each day.*
- *Save natural resources by recycling and buying recycled products.*
- *Drink tap water, or filter your own water at home.*
- *Whenever possible, limit your use of or do not use pesticides.*
- *If you eat seafood, make sustainable choices.*
- *Support your local farmers market.*
- *Get outside. Visit a park, volunteer, walk your dog, or ride your bike.*

Five years ago, Atlantic Publishing signed the Green Press Initiative. These guidelines promote environmentally friendly practices, such as using recycled stock and vegetable-based inks, avoiding waste, choosing energy-efficient resources, and promoting a no-pulping policy. We now use 100-percent recycled stock on all our books. The results: in one year, switching to post-consumer recycled stock saved 24 mature trees, 5,000 gallons of water, the equivalent of the total energy used for one home in a year, and the equivalent of the greenhouse gases from one car driven for a year.

Dedication

For Gabriel

Table of Contents

Chapter 2: Breaking Ground on the Basics 59

Chapter 3: Backyard Ponds 75

Chapter 4: Fountains............... 101

Chapter 5: Waterfalls...............115

Chapter 6: An Introduction to Water Gardening...... 131

Chapter 7: Swimming Under the Surface.................... 159

Chapter 8: Light It Up 185

Chapter 9: Care and Maintenance 195

Chapter 10: Happily Ever After.. 237

Introduction

There is a grain of truth in Aesop's fable for children about the country mouse and the city mouse. Each person feels a natural pull in his or her soul, toward the bright lights and fast pace of the city or the quiet air and open spaces of the country. In real life, it is not as simple as in the story. People choose city living for the opportunities available, the increased pace of life, the culture, and the social life.

Yet, the drawbacks to modern life, the traffic, the stress, the inevitable headaches, lead those same people to yearn for a return to the earth. Even the most seasoned city dweller appreciates time to get back to nature. Since the time of ancient civilizations, people have turned to water features to help them find this inner peace and tranquility. The soothing sound of a running stream or a calm spot for contemplation afforded by a bench overlooking a simple pond can be the perfect antidote to the hectic pace of life.

History of Water Features

Statue of Athena and Pallas in front of the Parliament Building
© Can Stock Photo Inc. / Ammit

Even in ancient times, humans celebrated water as more than just a source of life. Water also served to delight, beautify, and entertain. Just as we as a society are preoccupied with technological innovations, ancient society was delighted with fountains, which were the technological innovations of the day. Egyptians were known to have water fountains, which were accented around the edges with trees. There is even evidence that the Egyptians kept fish in these fountains. The Greeks built statuary fountains in the images of the gods and goddesses they revered. Ancient Roman and Middle Eastern people also kept water in their gardens in different designs. Romans created gravity-powered fountains with ornamental statues of an animal head.

In the Middle East, water had a presence in religious and non-religious designs. The sehan, or Islamic courtyard, traditionally included a certain water element. Religious designs dating back more than 1,000 years, such as The Great Mosque of Khairouan, a remarkably well-preserved mosque in Africa, included water in the form of a cleansing pool, for the incoming people to perform cleansing rituals. A pond was also found in the sehan to Middle Eastern homes. There, it served as a community gathering, an area to welcome guests, to drink coffee, and engage in a neighbor's hospitality.

In ancient Eastern cultures, the same water used to sustain and feed the earth was recognized as a salve for the soul. Much as the water kept the community going, it also kept the mind healthy and the soul stress-free. Chinese gardens in the classic style always include a water element with a fountain. In keeping with the Chinese design principles, all elements had to balance one another, and water was thought to balance out the harsher elements, such as rocks. The spray of the fountain and the arc of the water's movement were considered in the design.

Health and Wellness Benefits of Water Features

Adding a pond or a stream with a softly trickling waterfall can bring peace to your garden. Meditation, yoga, and simple contemplation can be made even more calming by the sound of a softly trickling waterfall.

Photo courtesy of Drs. Foster and Smith Aquatics

Chances are it has been awhile since you have thought about your health and even longer since you have considered your mental wellness. The damage stress can do to your body is significant. Studies have shown that your health can suffer as a result of taking on too much in your daily life. You might think stress is only costing you sleep. However, stress can lead to physical health problems, such as nausea, headaches, and even an erratic heartbeat. As simple as it might seem, gardening and spending time outside can help reduce your stress and improve your health. Those who suffer from mental health problems, such as depression or anxiety, can help themselves through increased exposure to sunlight and simple meditation.

If you have children, you have heard that childhood obesity is on the rise. You might have gotten pamphlets from the pediatrician's office or the school nurse suggesting a smarter diet and more exercise. But as every parent knows, children of a certain age cannot be forced to get outside. It is especially hard when they have television, computers, and video games at their disposal in the air-conditioned house. Throughout this guide, you will find suggestions for ways to involve your whole family in the process of building a pond. Start early by letting children help you design and site the pond. The more involved they are in the process from the beginning, the more time they will want to spend helping with and enjoying the new water feature.

How to Use This Guide to Plan Your Water Feature

Whether you hope to start small with a reservoir pond or revamp your whole backyard into a wildlife oasis, this guide can help you from inception to completion. Perhaps you picked it up out of curiosity. Installing a water feature might seem to be a major project and require more time and money than most homeowners are willing to invest. However, you might be surprised to learn that someone with an average skill level and limited experience can easily construct a backyard water feature with the right planning and supplies. By the time you have finished reading the book, you will have a complete picture of the planning, design, and work involved in a potential project.

The first two chapters will help you plan and prepare for the installation of a water feature. You will learn how to put together a design and a budget for your project. The next chapters provide a more in-depth look at each type of water feature. Chapter 3 details the process of constructing a backyard pond. Chapter 4 covers the different types of fountains you can construct. For those who are ready to tackle a larger project, Chapter 5 provides the necessary knowledge for constructing a waterfall.

After building this water feature, you might find you want to add a little something special to make it unique. The next part of the book covers extra additions to make your waterfall or fountain your own. Aspiring water gardeners can turn to Chapter 6 for an introduction to water gardening. Fish-lovers, flip to Chapter 7 for more information on adding fish to a water feature. Chapter 8 explains how even an amateur electrician can install lighting around a water feature.

The end of the book will guide you in taking care of your new water feature. Chapter 9 covers routine care and maintenance, while Chapter 10 gives a long-term outlook. Interspersed throughout the book, you will find design plans. These plans will give step-by-step instructions for each project, including the materials and time needed, the level of difficulty for a person of average skill and building knowledge, and how your final product should look. Use these plans, along with the advice and tips throughout the book, to make your dream landscape a reality.

CHAPTER 1

Designing an Oasis

A pond or fountain in the backyard seems like a good idea. Until it comes time to begin planning and your notepad remains blank. How do you even begin?

As in any situation, consulting with a professional is a good idea. If you have the means in your budget to hire a landscape designer, he or she will have the professional know-how to turn your idea into a reality. Prepare yourself for the first meeting with your landscape designer by collecting photos or design plans you found online or in magazines that resemble the feature you envision. This will help the designer understand the expectations you have and the style of feature you prefer. Reading this book also will help you in determining a design. As you read, you will learn more about the other factors that can influence your design, such as cost and amount of maintenance required.

What should you ask? Questions to ask your landscape designer at your initial meeting are:

- Is this design possible in my budget?
- Can you recommend a local professional to complete the project?
- What kinds of plants will thrive in our local climate?

- Can I add fish/more plants to this design at a later time? How many fish will this design accommodate?

- How much maintenance will this feature require?

Half the fun of undertaking a project like this is doing it yourself. The satisfaction of knowing you created something new with your own brain and hands, combined with the warm fuzzy feeling of receiving kudos from friends and family, makes it worth the effort. Or, perhaps you cannot afford to hire a professional. If this is the case, it is up to you to act as a designer. Although you might not have a wealth of design knowledge, you have your opinions and preferences, and they are valuable assets. Many styles and inspirations for a pond exist, and different cultures and architectural styles can inspire the pool. Though, any pond will fall into one of two styles:

- Formal: A pond styled to look more formal aims to look more like the classic style of French or Italian fountains and less like a natural pond. Formal-style ponds might have a raised edge that surrounds the pond area and are  more likely to include an elaborate fountain. Most formal ponds will include plants, strategically placed for design effect.

- Informal: A style inspired by nature and preferred by those who hope to create the kind of area that looks like a forest clearing. In nature, things are not planned and rigid, the way landscapes can be. The shape of your pond can have an influence on the look, so if you are hoping for a natural look, stay away from perfect geometric shapes, such as rectangles, squares, diamonds, or perfectly round circles. An informal look is better served with a simpler shape. Waterfalls in informal-style water features mimic those in nature, with rocks all around the slope. Connecting small ponds with a stream is another natural look. Surrounded by rocks and plants in bloom, the effect can be just like a forest stream.

Looking back at history to see which features appeal to you can be a good way to start turning your ideas into a design. Each architectural style has distinct components you can imitate in your plans. Even the features you do not like are worth taking note of, so you can eliminate certain styles that do not fit your vision.

Photo courtesy of Drs. Foster and Smith Aquatics

Planning your Backyard Vacation

Think how much time you spend planning a vacation: researching the destination, reading reviews of the hotels, finding activities for yourself and your family. And who can blame you? After all, you are spending your hard-earned money to visit this place, with the hopes that you will enjoy yourself, find a paradise on earth, and make memories for your family. These same considerations should be weighed when you consider your new water feature. After all, this will be your everyday vacation spot, the place you will come to get away. It will also be a large expense and one you should not take lightly. This is not much different than going on a vacation. You have to ask yourself, where would you like to go? Where will your escape take you? To an elegant traditional Chinese garden, where you can calmly drink tea? Will it be a woodland forest, with all the sights and sounds of nature? Perhaps a Mediterranean getaway, where the cool blue tiles will reflect the water's light back at you?

Figure out where you want to go first, and then figure out why. Is it the bright, sun-splashed colors and terra-cotta clay accents of a Mediterranean look that appeal to you? Is it the formal lines and clean look of an urban-inspired waterfall?

There are many places you can go as long as you study and isolate what aspect of that style pleases you. Is it the color scheme used? Is it the size and placement of the fountain? Here are examples of times and places you could visit in your personal paradise:

Go Ancient

Think of a soft, sandy beach with the sea so blue that it almost hurts your eyes with its power; a city so far ahead of its time that long after the people are gone, new generations will speak of them in awe; and voices surrounding the sound of a trickling fountain. These are the voices of a philosopher that explain the true meaning of life: a merchant haggling the price of his wares and women gossiping under their breath as they collect the water to sustain their families. In ancient cultures, the water fountain was a place to gather, to talk, to sing a song, or to hear a thought.

If you aspire to imitate the ancients, keep in mind the duality of ancient design. Although the water fountain was a feature designed to add beauty and enjoyment to the area, it also served a purpose. In ancient Greece, the large community fountain, known as the fountain house, was where the women of the community would fetch water. A fountain that hopes to look like an ancient fountain cannot be too ornate. It must also give the impression of functionality so visitors can envision the lines of women dipping their clay pots under the surface. The ancient Greeks used simple materials, such as plaster, limestone, and granite, in their designs. Metals were then used to add shine and decorative elements to the feature. A simple-styled, neutrally colored water feature can mesh with different architectural styles, so it will look good in the yard of different homes. If you are hoping for an old look, statuary fountains can be purchased in different finishes, some made to look aged. But, if you are handy with a paintbrush, you can purchase plain statuary and paint accents on the statue and surrounding pool edge.

Go Renaissance Italian

Trevi Fountain in Rome

Picture your backyard the way it is now, perhaps unremarkable and the same as every other yard in the neighborhood. Now, picture it as a makeshift trattoria, an Italian-style café. Old-style brick pavers line the area around the water. A statuary fountain, perhaps of a beautifully sculpted man or a gently weeping goddess, gives off a fine mist into the summer air. Tile-topped café-style tables surround the splashing water. Friends can toss coins into the water and see if your fountain's luck brings them true love. The smell of brewing espresso and the sound of accordion music are what you need to make the Italian feel complete. At night, spotlights illuminate the statue to give the yard a romantic feel, perfect for dancing under the stars. With simple steps, you can return to the romantic locations of a cherished vacation.

Many the water features featured throughout Italy were created during the renaissance, and these inspired modern fountains in several cultures. Renaissance fountains were statuaries, a fountain with an ornamental statue, from which the water flows. In Rome, fountains were created in past times to provide water for the people or as a tribute to someone. In one square alone, the Piazza Navona, there are three fountains. Rome's grandest fountain, the Trevi Fountain, features sculptures of a sea king and sea nymphs and still brings scores of tourists, especially on hot summer days. The mythical power of the Trevi fountain has inspired songs and movies, all about people hoping to be fortunate enough to return there.

The history behind these pieces is equally inspiring. The fountains of Rome were originally powered by gravity. The architects who designed them had to figure the distance and elevation of the source water for the fountain to determine the type of spray they could anticipate. The spirit of the Renaissance pieces vary, from fun and whimsical to serious works of art.

If you hope to create a feature that invokes this spirit, think about a statuary in a faux marble finish, or purchase a plain statuary and create your own finish using nontoxic, waterproof paint. Gold Leaf can be applied in a seemingly random pattern to give the impression of a gold finish that has worn away over time.

Example of a design that has had Gold Leaf applied to it

Go French

Sacré Coeur in Paris, France

There are classic pieces of French architecture you are familiar with, but architectural styles and features exist beyond the Eiffel Tower and Cathedral de Notre Dame. French Romanesque architecture used a simpler, less ornamental styling than is normally associated with the French. This style was simpler, with less statues, large arches, and thick walls. Unless you are hoping to emulate a Romanesque style, opulence is key when it comes to going French.

French gothic architecture had a more elaborate styling than the Romanesque, with pillars, spires and gargoyles imposing on the viewer from the outside. It was during this period that the flying buttress, a kind of arch and pillar support seen on the Notre Dame Cathedral and Sacré Coeur, was invented. This allowed the architect to build higher and more grandiose structures.

Next, during the renaissance times, the French took the Italian style to another level by adding more adornment. French-styled features were designed to be ostentatious and made of expensive-looking materials, such as marble or gold. Famous gardens, such as the ones at Versailles, were constructed with waterways and fountains intertwined to encourage long walks with the classic French companion, un petit chien (a little dog). Elaborate to the point of gaudiness, but not apologetic, French styling during this time was designed to catch the eye and impress the viewer.

Even if elaborate is not your style, there are other inspirations to take from the French. Consider a recent construction, the glass pyramid at the Louvre, renowned American architect I.M. Pei conceived. The pyramid sits in the courtyard area. Next to the pyramid, fountains shoot high into the air. The reflection of the water off the glass pyramid makes the fountain even more enjoyable. In the same way, consider what you could place in your fountain's foreground or background to accentuate the spray.

Go Urban Contemporary

Not every lake or pond is peaceful and tranquil. The water borders a vibrant city and pulses with energy. In other cities, there is no natural shoreline but still plenty of waterfront to observe. Urban dwellers do not exist in a concrete maze. In major cities, an eye-catching water feature serves to draw passersby. In a strange way, the urban water feature is similar to the ancient water feature. Walk by a fountain in a local park or in the courtyard between two office buildings on a busy day. Mothers will be gathered around, watching their children run around the fountain. Business people will bark orders into their cellphones as they try to soak up sun. Buskers will strum a guitar, or pound on a makeshift drum, and sing for their supper. In the same way that water was a gathering place for us back then, it remains one to this day.

No better example exists of this than Central Park, where the beautiful lakes, ponds, and fountain are man made and strategically planned to give visitors maximum enjoyment. In recent years, cities have seen the need to add more water to their landscapes. In Toronto, Canada,

Aerial photo of Central Park in New York City

construction is ongoing on the largest urban revitalization project in North America, the city's new waterfront. When finished, the project will include

90 parks and public spaces along the waterfront. Urban style features have thought-out viewing areas, with ample seating and lighting. For those who prefer a more contemporary look, cleaner lines and modern materials are needed. Concrete, glass, and lighting are used to dramatic effect in these features.

Go Asian

To those unfamiliar with the differing styles of the Chinese, Japanese, and other cultures, the word Asian lumps together many styles of feature. Koi ponds, rock gardens, and Zen gardens come to mind. In truth, these elements belong to the Chinese and Japanese styles.

© Can Stock Photo Inc. / rramirez125

Traditional Chinese gardens are composed of many elements, each placed in relation and harmony to the others. Any homeowner who aspires to add a Chinese-inspired garden should first spend time familiarizing themselves with the art of feng shui, a classic Chinese discipline. Although water factors into a Chinese garden, it must factor in a way that is harmonious to the other elements.

Japanese gardens feature water and a bridge spanning the water, or stepping stones across the water. Stones or rocks also are featured prominently in Japanese gardens and comprise whole gardens of their own. Traditional Zen gardens are the only kind of traditional Japanese gardens that do not feature water but feature rocks or sand instead. The water feature in traditional Japanese gardens is meant to look as natural as possible. The plants should also be a natural leafy green.

Feng shui

The name of this old Chinese art literally translates to "wind" and "water," but it encompasses more than those two elements. Feng shui focuses on the orientation of elements together to reach a harmonious balance. Said to take its roots in Chinese astrology, the art itself dates back thousands of years. Feng shui began in the West Han dynasty in about the 3rd century B.C. The simplest aim of feng shui is to achieve the balance between heaven and earth that provides a positive Qi, a type of energy. Qi is said to be the significant force or energy on people's lives. Feng shui assesses the orientation of a structure or feature and how to encourage its harmony with the surrounding environment including the local climate and vegetation. The feature is placed where it cannot block the energy of the other elements.

Throughout time, feng shui has spread from China to the Western world. Many U.S. companies have begun redesigning their headquarters and offices to better reflect the principles of feng shui. Amateurs and regular decorators might try to apply what they know about feng shui for you. But if you truly hope to follow the guidelines of feng shui, the best way to learn is to read up on the principles or to ask an expert to analyze the site for you. Inform yourself about the cardinal direction your house faces and the area where you want the pond to sit.

Go Mediterranean

Mediterranean style conjures up a vision of shallow courtyard pools finished in blue and white tiles, standing out under the blustering sunshine. But many structures in the ancient civilizations surrounding the Mediterranean were constructed in natural stones and date back to the ancient times. Intricate tile work, with small, ornate designs, is featured. This style is known for textured, aged-looking surfaces, and bright, earth-colored accents. Add terra-cotta pieces and brass urns, and you have yourself a day on the Mediterranean beach.

Here again, as with Asian style, the term is used as a catchall. Although the term Mediterranean is thrown around to describe one style, it encompasses many. The term Mediterranean refers to the style of a particular region of the world. The countries surrounding the Mediterranean Sea, such as Turkey, Greece, and Egypt, are those of a warmer climate. Mediterranean ponds are typified as shallow, tiled ponds without many plants or adornments. Because some of these countries are Muslim countries, they might be sehans, or Islamic courtyards. Although Mediterranean design might be simple with its clean lines, it is rarely informal. Pools in a geometric shape with a raised edge are more popular. Mediterranean-styled features do not incorporate plants in them, and what plants do appear are well-kept and carefully manicured.

Other design decisions

Having decided on a style of inspiration, next turn your attention to local concerns. Learning about the plants available to you and those that flourish in your local climate can help you avoid problems in the future. It also will keep your feature from looking out of place. Blending the style that inspires you with local plants will go a long way toward creating a unique feature of your own.

The best way to study up on nature is to turn off the computer and get outside. Local or community gardens contain a water feature you can observe up close. Observe the placement of the feature in the garden space and take note of the possible reasons why it was placed this way. Does this spot afford multiple viewing areas from which the water can be seen? Is there ample shade from a nearby tree or structure?

This is also an opportunity to use your other senses to determine what you want in your own backyard. If the feature has a fountain or waterfall, take note of the level of noise it makes. Do you want the water in your waterfall to fall at the same rate so it makes a similar sound? Are you hoping for the peaceful sound of a soft trickle or the constant burble of flowing water? These preferences will help you decide what equipment to buy later.

A community garden is also a good place to volunteer and learn how to care for a pond before breaking ground on your own. The other people you meet might be valuable resources because they can offer tips only gardeners familiar with your local climate  will know. They can suggest plants that will thrive in your pond, and you can observe how quickly the suggested plants spread in the pond area.

Another valuable resource can be a local pond, stream, or lake. Even if you are going for a more formal, landscaped look, you do not want your feature to look awkward or alien in your backyard. Looking at a natural (not man made) pond or lake can help you gather ideas about how to make the feature look natural and make it fit in the surroundings. Study the natural placement of bushes and shrubs, the way rock outcroppings are composed, or how a stream snakes across the forest floor. Look at the colors present in the local plants and decide if they fit the color scheme you have planned for your pond. Use these observations to help when selecting plants and rocks for the edges of the feature and putting them together.

Additional resources

Living in the information age has its benefits. You can find help, tips, and support groups online for new and inexperienced gardeners. Local farmers, gardeners, and nurseries will keep blogs full of valuable tips and resources. When you are ready to purchase your equipment, read the reviews for the pieces you anticipate purchasing on pond supply store websites. Home improvement stores offer seasonal seminars that give crash courses in different aspects of renovation.

When you grab the notepad again and take another crack at planning your backyard masterpiece, consider the architectural style you prefer and why. Try to figure out what specifically draws you to that style. Is it the lines and shapes used to create the water flow? The colors and materials that stand out? The styling of the work?

Last, take time to consider the style of your home. Is an Asian-inspired koi pond going to clash with the styling of your home? Consider whether you live in a simple, contemporary home with clean lines or an elegant

Victorian with plenty of adornment. If you want your backyard to be a different style than your home, think about how you will transition from one to the other. If you have a larger yard, perhaps you can create a path or walkway leading to the area to give the visitor a clear feeling that a new area is beginning.

CASE STUDY: ADDING A PIECE OF PARADISE

Richard Ventola
President
Green Acres Inc.
www.greenacresinc.com

Having a properly installed pond at one's home is like having a piece of paradise in your own yard; no need to travel to find that nice little feel-good, peaceful spot to relax. It can be right outside your door. The four seasons only enhance the experience of having a pond as you get to see the changes occur. From water lilies to ice formations, it is all beautiful.

You improve a person's quality of life when you build them a beautiful water feature. When I added water features to our list of specialty services, I saw a different reaction from my customers. They no longer were casual customers. They were friends. The water features would create a bond unlike anything we have ever done before. When I finished my first water feature, I received my first hug and tears of joy from a customer. Since then, I have made friends, received hugs, and realized that this type of work gives my life a more meaningful purpose than I could have ever imagined.

I am a Certified Aquascape Contractor with 24 years of experience in the art of installing water features. The technology and materials have changed dramatically over the years. We understand the ecosystem required to have a healthy pond, and if you follow those principals when building one, you will have a low-maintenance, beautiful water feature.

I am required to attend seminars every year to keep up on the latest improvements in the industry. This includes classes on koi health, aquatic plants, regulations, and new trends in the industry. Because I do this as a profession, I do not need help, but if I do, it is only a phone call away. The Aquascape method is the best because it mimics what is found in Mother Nature. The pond should contain rocks, fish, plants, and mechanical filtration.

I have two ponds at my home. One is in the front of the house and contains about 40 koi and aquatic plants. The one in the rear of my home contains about a dozen larger koi and aquatic plants. I do not see any drawbacks other than when you lose one of your prize koi. The benefit is that you can find peace and beauty in your own yard, which is priceless. Take a pond tour in your area and see the possibilities.

A common mistake people make is not making the pond big enough and then as soon as it is done, they say, "I wish it were bigger." The average pond owner rebuilds his or her pond three times to make it bigger.

Do not wait any longer. Jump in and get your feet wet.

Expect the unexpected

Although the cost and time needed for your project can be planned, there will be unexpected difficulties. A water feature, especially one that strives to include fish and plants, is not unlike any other new addition to the family: Even as it gives you joy, it will require much from you. Common problems to be ready for:

- A new pond might require being filled, emptied, and refilled several times as part of the filling process.

- A pond newly stocked with fish requires constant observation and water testing. This can require everyday attention.

- Excavation might be too taxing for you to complete with a shovel, and you might need to rent equipment to dig the pond.

- Any dirt excavated to make your pond that you cannot reuse in the feature, such as in a slope for the waterfall, will need to be disposed of or repurposed. If you have a green thumb, consider starting a compost heap with the dirt. If you cannot find a way to repurpose the dirt, you might wind up having to pay for removal.

- Seasonal maintenance will require extra time from you each spring and fall to prepare for heavy use in the summer and disassembly or hibernation in the winter.

Observing your pond, especially if it is a fish pond, is one of the quickest and easiest ways to identify problems or changes that need to be made. The appearance of the water, plants, and fish can tell you about their conditions. Plan to spend time around your pond after it is completed. As you observe your pond, behavioral patterns will begin to emerge from your fish and plants. This will help you get familiar with the usual conditions of the pond and make it easier for you to spot things that go amiss. Even small changes to the ecosystem can affect the pond, so take note of any changes to the water level or flow.

Investing Your Time and Money

Having determined the style that suits you, another important factor is the budget available for your project. If you have a larger budget, use it wisely to make the process of creating a water feature easier on yourself.

Renting equipment to dig the pond area and move the dirt out of the way does not cost much, and it makes one of the physically taxing parts of the process easier. Also, think about spending more to get more in the long run. Choosing equipment of higher quality will help you get the most value for your money because it will require fewer repairs through the years.

Creativity can help you budget for the oasis you want if your funds are not as plentiful. If you are willing to do the labor yourself, a project can be created on a small budget. Even better, you already have the basic garden tools needed for the excavation, such as a shovel, spade, and wheelbarrow. The specific parts needed for a water feature can be purchased in any price range. *These parts are discussed in more detail later in the chapters devoted to each feature.* Cost-effective plants can be purchased or snipped for free from a friend with a green thumb. More lavish plants can be purchased and added later if you still feel they are needed for the look of the area. When adding a more complicated feature, such as a fountain or a waterfall, the budget required can be much larger than for a pond. A pump or fountainhead can be purchased cheaply, but quality is a concern because you will use your feature. Having a pump wear out before it should and having to extract and replace it can turn out to be more expensive in the end.

Equal consideration must be given to how much time you can devote to the project. A simple garden pond can be constructed and filled in the spare time available during a weekend, with only a little ongoing care. This type of pond is an easy way to gradually begin introducing water to your landscape and your schedule. As you find more time to devote to the backyard oasis, the pond can be modified to include fish, which would transform a simple garden pond into a fish pond; or a bog, a marshy area where plants are left untamed, can be added to the margins of the pond for a more natural look. Other projects will require more time up front and less as time goes on. A fountain or waterfall will take more time to prepare and construct. But ongoing care, including routine maintenance of the filter, is less involved than the water monitoring and testing required for a pond where living things grow.

Keeping Your Invited Visitors Safe and Involved

There are drawbacks for you to consider before starting. For those who have children or pets, safety is an issue. Although a backyard water feature is not likely to be deep, the addition of water to an environment where children play presents a safety concern. There are, however, precautions you can take while planning and constructing the pond. Consider the ages of the children as you plan. Placing the water feature in an area farther away from the house can help because children will have a hard time getting to it quickly. This might buy you time if a child gets away from you. However, it will take you longer to reach the pond from your house if, for example, you look out your window and spot a child wandering toward it.

Adding a form of edging that creates a barrier between children and the water, such as logs, a fence, or a bridge, is a good start. If the children are a little older, you might find that edging is enough. Those wanting a more foolproof solution will find that as with backyard pools, the secure option is to install a fence around the area. This option, though it might be worthwhile for those concerned with safety, might ruin the viewing area and sight lines to the area.

Talking to your children can also help. Explain to them that this pond is not a swimming pool and the reasons why they must stay out of the water. If your pond is a home for fish, you can try to explain that this is their environment, no different than the tank or bowl they would be kept in indoors.

~~~~~~

Attractive nuisance

Although the addition of a pond to your garden might add value to your home, it might also add to your insurance premium. Check with your homeowner's insurance to see if your water feature constitutes an attractive nuisance — insurance agent speak for something that draws the attention of children while presenting a danger to them. You as a homeowner might be liable for any accidents that happen, so be sure to supervise visitors and keep them from playing on the edging around your pond. Do not avoid notifying the insurance company because the failure to do so might be reason enough for them to terminate your coverage. Worse yet, the insurance company can deny unrelated claims because of you withholding this information.

~~~~~~

As long as your children are old enough to understand and be trusted around a small pond, this can be an opportunity to teach them outdoor skills. It can also help to get them off the couch and away from the TV. If your hope is to foster a green thumb in your children, there are ways you can get them involved in the pond.

Child-Friendly Pond Activities for any Ages

Water Feature	Time of year	Activity
Plants	Spring/ Summer	Plant and care for your own greenery. This can be a fun project for summer vacation visits because children will have a chance to see the plants progress, and you will have a way to get them outside every day. This can also be a way to get children interested in helping with care and maintenance of the pond area.
Pond	Anytime	Have children help you perform routine water testing on the pond. Children will enjoy helping with the water testing, as long as they are old enough to be trusted not to drink the water from the specimen cups.
Pond	Anytime	Older children can be introduced to the idea of an ecosystem and taught about the creatures and plants that make up your pond. Keeping an observation journal is a fun activity that will encourage other creative activities, such as drawing plants and fish.
Fish	Anytime	Fish care and feeding can be a good way to introduce responsibility to younger children or measure whether an older child is ready for a more taxing pet.
Any feature	Holidays	Incorporate the pond area into the holidays with children. Easter egg hunts and jack-o'-lantern carving can be done pond side. Have children help decorate the pond in holiday decors. Try hanging a tire from a nearby tree to create the look of an old-fashioned water hole for the Fourth of July. The finished pond will make a background for family photos that document the growth of the pond plants and the children.

Keeping animals out can be just as important as keeping children out. Certain animals will destroy plants. Others will destroy the pond's edging and liner. Fish keepers have a whole other set of worries. Animals like a free meal, and many of them would love to feast on your pond fish. Curious household pets can be counted on to swipe a paw at the fish. Other small animals, such as raccoons and birds, will also try to eat your fish. To protect animal visitors from the water, or protect your fish from them, a net can be installed under the water's surface or suspended above it. This will ruin the visual effect of the pond somewhat, but if you have spent a large amount of money on fancy fish, it might be necessary.

Creating a place for your fish to hide from attack on the bottom of the pond will also help. Think of the skulls and plastic castles you see in aquariums, only larger. Unlike the aquarium versions, which tend to be in neon colors, these hiding places must camouflage well with the pond bottom. It is aesthetically better not to be able to see these, but it will also help to deter swimming or diving predators. Even if a heron cannot reach the fish, if it can see a brightly colored area the fish are hiding inside, it might spend all day stalking and diving on the surface of your pond. A hollow log, another aquarium favorite, is a good option.

Inviting animals in

Are you hoping to draw animals in rather than drive them away? Here are things you can do:

- Install a bird feeder in or around the pond area.

- Create an easy access point for animals to enter, such as a beach area on one side of the pond. A gradual slope built into one side of the pond can be covered with gravel, sand, or pebbles to create a beach. This will create an area for the animals to bathe or drink easily.

- Consider plants that certain animals, birds, and insects will seek out as food. *The appendix at the end of this guide provides information on the plants that double as food for animal visitors.*

- Leave the animals that naturally wander to the pond to familiarize themselves. Unless you fear an animal to be harmful or destructive, leave it to get comfortable in your pond's environment.

Winterizing Your Pond

Living in a colder climate where the summer can be fleeting means you are determined to enjoy the summer nights in the backyard while you can. Is it worth it to install a pond if you can only enjoy it for a few months of the year? It depends on how much you value the memories of hot summer nights spent drinking a cold beverage with friends next to the pond.

Winterizing the feature does not have to be complicated as long as you anticipate your coming winter. In the coldest climates, a pond that uses equipment, such as a pump or filter, will need to be drained and the equipment cleaned and stored away. In climates where the winter is milder, the pond can be left to freeze as long as it does not freeze entirely into a solid. Get familiar with your pond plants and what climate they prefer. If you are not sure which plants are recommended to last through the winter, talk to local gardeners or your local garden supply store.

You can also check the U.S. Department of Agriculture's (USDA) Plant Hardiness map. *This map can be found in Chapter 6.* This map will classify your location into a zone based on the lowest known temperature in your region. You can use this information to find out which plants can reliably be expected to survive the winter outdoors. Tropical plants will have to come inside. Be sure to place them where they can drink in sunlight while waiting to go back outside. Tougher plants can be moved to a deeper location in the pond to survive.

A pond that is also home to fish must be emptied in the colder climates and the fish transferred to an aquarium. In locations where the pond is not likely to freeze all the way through, the fish can stay because they are able to survive under the frozen surface. Because pond fish do not have a stomach, if they are going to be fed in colder temperatures, they need lower protein food to digest it. After the temperature drops to less than 60 degrees, do not feed the fish regular food. Once the temperature drops another 10 degrees, stop feeding the fish altogether. Those unsure about how severe the coming winter will be should err on the side of caution because trying to melt the ice or break the frozen surface of a pond can harm and traumatize fish. You can purchase a pond de-icer, which will ensure a hole stays in the top of the pond as it freezes. This hole will allow any gases the fish produce, such as carbon monoxide, to escape. If you choose to install an air pump or aerator, winter is a good time to run this pump to ensure your fish have enough oxygen.

Over time, it is possible that your water feature will spring a leak. As long as time and care are taken while installing the feature, leaks should be a minimal concern. The leaks that do spring up can easily be patched, and you can buy patch kits at the local store.

Placing Your Feature

Figuring out where your feature should go on the property is another decision that might seem complicated. You might want to take the time to do sketches of your available yard space with the water feature in different locations. You can also do a "sketch" in the yard by drawing out the shape of your water feature on the grass using chalk or nontoxic paint. More technically inclined homeowners might want to create a site plan to scale of the property.

Those who are not artistically inclined enough to create a site plan by hand can use computer programs. You might already have Microsoft Paint installed on your computer, which you can use to make a rough design. Use the geometric shapes provided in the program to mark the area occupied by your house, driveway, or shed if you do not have much practice drawing with the mouse. For a more professional looking plan, Google offers a free 3-D modeling software called SketchUp (**http://sketchup.google.com**). SketchUp allows you to create a realistic and detailed plan in a 3-D animation style. Professional architects and landscape designers use SketchUp because the plan can be made to measurements specified by the user. Many garden designs created with SketchUp's technology are available to view online. You can use these as another source of inspiration. Specialized programs designed for designing and positioning backyard ponds are also available for purchase online. If you choose to buy a landscape or garden design program, look for one that offers a 3-D walk around. This will offer you an animated view of what it will look like as you tour the finished product.

Enjoy the view

A main reason for adding a water feature is the view. When planning where the feature should go, consider the ways you hope to view it. Will you be spending your outdoor time after work when the light is minimal? Consider placing your pond where it will get the most lingering sunlight. Do you hope to view your pond from inside your home, whether from a window or through a sliding glass door? Then your feature will have to be situated where you can see it from that place. If you hope to have a hidden effect where the feature is not immediately visible from the main entry point to the yard, this will require the right placement and landscaping.

Go with what nature gave you

Here, it is better to follow Mother Nature's lead. Consider the natural lighting on the property at different times of the day, especially at the times you will be likely to view the pond. The light and length of day will vary based on the time of year, so keep in mind how much things will change over the course of the year as you plan.

In the summertime, your water feature is no different from you: it has to get just the right amount of sunlight. If your pond gets too much sunlight and gets too warm in the summer, the pond will require constant refilling as the water evaporates. This is wasteful, costly, and time consuming. Introducing new, chemically treated hose water into your pond will upset the ecological balance you have spent time creating and will require monitoring and possibly even chemical treatment to restore each time.

But placing your pond too far in the shade creates problems of its own. If you hope to encourage plants to grow in the first place, you have to ensure the pond gets a certain amount of sun: about six hours per day. For the best results from your pond, the water temperature needs to stay consistent.

Making it too hot, too cold, or simply making too many changes to the water will make it harder for things to grow harmoniously.

Use your dips and slopes to your advantage

Next, consider the lay of your land. Does the yard have a natural slope? It is important to consider this in the placement of your feature. For creating a waterfall or running stream, this natural slope can be useful. You might want to consider working with it to get the maximum effect with the minimum amount of work.

On the other hand, situating the pond part of your water feature at the bottom of the slope is not a good idea. Rain or lawn irrigation will run water into your pond, which will upset the water's balance and bring in dirt and pebbles. If you use chemical pesticides or fertilizer, it might not be good for the plants or fish in the pond to have the yard's rainwater drain into the pond. Even simple dirt and grass clippings will upset the water's chemistry as they decompose, which will make more work for you in the long run.

Anything that can drop from a tree or bush, whether it is fruit, a nut, a leaf, or a flower, will have the same effect on the pond's water. For this reason, if the slope of your yard is steep and there is yard debris to be caught in the pond, it might be best to situate your pond above the slope. If you still choose to place your feature at the bottom of the slope, creating a raised edge or lip along the perimeter of the pool can help to keep undesirable debris from washing into the pool.

Get it out of the way

After considering the natural elements, consider the current state of your yard. Your pond will last a long time, and placing it in a site you are not happy with can be a costly mistake. Moving other things that exist in the yard might seem like unnecessary work, but consider their  permanence versus the pond's. Existing shrubbery, trees, or small structures, such as children's play equipment, might need to be moved or removed to accommodate the best views and location for your water feature.

More permanent fixtures will have to play into your design as well. A tree near your pond can give pleasant shade for a viewing area, but it will also shed leaves and other things into the pond water beneath it, which can upset the balance of your pond water and force you to clean the pond more than is necessary. Do not forget that the tree will need root space, so you cannot plant too close. The roots of a tree can fight and win against any kind of man made liner pond.

Avoid the power and pipes

Another concern is obtaining the necessary permits and permissions. You will have to check where the power lines are on your property; the local power company will be happy to come out and mark them for you. It might take time for them to send a representative to your property, though, so call well ahead of the date you plan to dig and install the pond.

Any pond that hopes to have an electrical component, such as a pump or lighting, will need to be close enough to the house for a power cable to reach it. Although longer power cables are available, installation and future repairs can be made easier by using a shorter cable. For an inexperienced electrician, using an extra long cord will be more difficult, especially if it turns out to be too long for the allotted space. If the city or county where you live requires permitting, they might also require zoning, which means they might also want to know about or approve the feature's location on the property.

You might have to submit a site plan of your property that shows the proposed location. Depending on their requirements, a professional might need to prepare or sealed and stamped this. This might delay your schedule because you cannot begin until you get the go-ahead from them. The process of getting the appropriate paperwork together, submitting it, and waiting for the green light can take weeks, and you might find yourself impatient to begin, but rushing is inadvisable. Many counties will send an inspector to view the property, and if the inspector sees work already under way, he or she will be forced to shut you down. Penalties and fines might follow. Planning for any legal delay can save you unnecessary headaches and even expense.

Stay friends with your neighbors

Unless you live on a large property, your neighbors will also be a concern when placing your feature. Even if you have a fence, your new feature could still upset your neighbors. In any feature where water is displaced, there will be splashing sounds. The sound from the pump powering the feature will be even louder. You might find the sound soothing and pleasant, but your neighbors might find it annoying and obnoxious.

If you have a smaller yard, your neighbors will likely be able to hear the feature no matter where you place it. The best way to handle this might be a head-on approach. Let your neighbors know you have added a waterfall or fountain, and commit to a reasonable time each night that you will turn the equipment off. In a larger yard, site the feature so it is away from the neighbors or at least as far away from their house as possible, so they are not disturbed.

The wind at certain times of the year can be strong enough to push the water from a fountain out of the pond and into a neighbor's yard. There is not much you can do about this if you live in a windy climate, but installing a buffer to protect the feature from the wind's power might help. Consider a fence, a seating area, or a hedge, but keep in mind a hedge will add to your cleanup. The wind will blow the leaves into the pond, and you will have to fish them out before they can affect your pond's water. Also, consider what you know about your yard. One part of the yard gets more wind than the rest, just as one part of the yard gets more sun than any other. The location of your home might affect the wind pattern in the yard; it might block the wind or even create a slight wind tunnel in places. You can use basic tools, such as a simple windsock, to see if the area directly behind your house is receiving less wind and, if so, how much less. Simply place a windsock, tied to a stake on the ground, in the area behind the house and another in an area to the side of the house. Then observe the amount of wind passing through each in any given day.

Create a viewing area

You might want to create a special viewing area later, so leave room for this. If you hope to add a bench for soaking up the sun while you read a book or observe and feed wildlife, consider which side of the pond will receive more sun, and leave enough space for this area on that side. If you hope to have a table and chairs where your family can eat lunch or dinner, it might be better to have shade to sit in, especially if you live in a hot or sunny climate. If you have created a beach along one side, consider a grassy area for seating and observation.

Incorporating special occasions

If you already have a special event planned, consider incorporating your new landscape. Backyard weddings are popular for a couple looking to stay in a certain budget. With the amount of design choices available, a backyard wedding can be designed to complement a couple's style on the big day. Also, having a picturesque location to take pictures saves you the trouble of having to trot your bridal party around a public park or garden.

Consider the atmosphere you can create by changing the backyard landscape. Unless you have the money to drape a hotel ballroom or hall in fabric, there is not a practical way to change the color of a rented location. But the garden area can easily provide a neutral canvas for or complement the bride's desired color scheme. Flowers are one of the biggest expenses when it comes to wedding decor. Planting blooms that match the bride's colors ensures the right colors are featured without the added work of creating and placing arrangements. Nature will do this part of the work for you.

You can also influence the yard's color scheme by adding planters in any color. Pond lights and spotlights can be used to illuminate the water feature in almost any color. Unlike any indoor locale, your guests can bask in the garden smells, fresh flowers, and cool breezes. Even a bride who has a high-concept theme for her wedding in mind can manage to make this concept real with creativity.

- For an Asian-themed wedding to whisk guests off to the Far East, create a rock garden with a small footbridge painted an eye-catching red, or have a traditionally styled pagoda built. Add lanterns around the pond in the classic Japanese style. Guests can observe and perhaps feed the koi as they mingle.

- A Cinderella-themed wedding needs a palace garden. A formally styled ceremony can be conducted in the area in front of a well-manicured statuary fountain. Neatly trimmed hedges and rosebushes in bloom complement a lush look, and small outdoor lights can be strung around trees to give a romantic ambiance.

- Have a stay-at-home destination wedding. Add a pebble beach to the edges of your pond, complete with seashells. Bring in tiki torches or pillar candles inside hurricane lamps, and greet the guests with leis. Bright, tropical plants and a natural-style waterfall can help transport the guests into your vision.

Design Project No. 1: A Container Pond

Photo courtesy of Drs. Foster and Smith Aquatics

Are you anxious to begin bringing a little water to your yard? Planning a water feature takes time, and rushing to begin is not a good idea. Instead, consider taking on a small project. A reservoir or container pond is an easy project to do in an afternoon. These are also known as accent or decorative ponds. It will help you get familiar with the tools and processes you will use later to construct a large pond. Depending on the size of the container you choose, you can use this little project in many places. It can be set out front as a seasonal porch decoration or kept in the backyard to create more of a water area near the pond.

Step One: Choose a Container

This type of pond can be made in any type of container. Garden planters, silver barrels, whiskey barrels or even a large vase can work. Home improvement or craft stores might sell decorative pools intended for just this purpose. You can be creative and select any container you would like as long as you are only planning to float a few plants in it. If you intend to put fish in this pond, though, you will have to consider their needs. Even one or two fish require a minimum amount of space. At least 10 gallons is advisable for keeping fish, but check with the store you purchased your fish from to see how much water each specific breed will need.

Step Two: Waterproof the Container

If you are sure your container is already waterproof, with no holes for drainage, you are ready to go. If your container has holes or cracks, you will need to make the container waterproof. A larger container, such as a whiskey barrel, can be lined with the same type of flexible liner used to line a pond or a cheaper polyurethane substitute. Specialty retailers offer pre-molded liners in shapes that fit directly in standard-sized barrels, with a lip on one side that slopes to create a waterfall effect. A smaller container, such as a planter or vase, can be painted with waterproof paint from the local hardware or craft store. Make sure the paint is not toxic, and let a few days pass before filling the container with water. Even then, it is a good idea to fill the container and dump the water out a few times before filling it for good.

Step Three: Fill the Container

If you are using a large container, it might become too heavy to lift and move around. Try placing the prepared but empty container in different areas around your yard. Place it in the final spot before filling it. Water lilies or other floating plants can add a nice finishing touch to the look of the pond if it is deep enough. Floating votive candles are available in almost every color and shape. A rubber duck floating in the pond adds a whimsical touch. This same pond can later be turned into a fountain with a few modifications. *See Chapter 4 on fountains for details on how to do this.*

MORE SMALL PROJECTS

- Create and decorate your own stepping stones for the area around the pool. You can personalize a design, such as a family crest or a child's handprint, or opt for a funkier, mosaic design. Kits with the items you need to design stepping stones are available at craft stores. If you are comfortable working with cement, you can purchase a mold to make your own stepping stones from scratch.

- Small statues made of cement or concrete for around the pool area can be purchased at home improvement or craft stores in a plain finish. You can then use craft paint to make them your own.

CHAPTER 2

~~~~~~~~~~~~~~~~~~~~~~~~~~~~~~~~~~~

Breaking Ground
on the Basics

Having decided what kind of water feature your yard needs, you might be tempted to toss your notepad to the side, run to get the supplies, and break ground before the sun goes down. However, this is a costly and foolish approach. Taking time to prepare your project will make the installation go more smoothly. Before venturing any further with your idea, learn about the supplies and materials you will need.

Supplies

To begin, you will need the supplies that might seem obvious but are the easiest to forget. Depending on the size of your pond and how you choose to approach the excavation, you might need gardening gloves, a shovel, a spade, and a wheelbarrow. Or, you might choose to rent an excavator or hire someone to excavate the site for you. Do not forget to plan what you will do with the excavated dirt. If you will be creating a waterfall to go with your feature, the dirt can be used to create a slope in which to place the waterfall. If you cannot repurpose the dirt, check to see if it can be disposed on your regular trash day. You will likely have to haul it to a dump or a friend's compost heap.

~~~~~~

Do not forget to ask

It is your responsibility to check with local authorities to see if a permit is required for the changes you hope to make. A small pond should not require a permit, but if you choose to add lighting, a wall, or a bridge, the requirements might be different. Call your city or county government's planning department to find out what forms you need to file. Although it might seem like a pain, the consequences of not having the right permit are much worse.

~~~~~~

Project-Specific Materials

Next, you will need the materials specific to your project. Even if you aspire to have a waterfall or fountain, you will still begin with a pond to place it in.

Liners

The first thing, and one of the most important things, needed for a pond is a liner, a watertight seal that separates the water from the earth. The volume and weight of the water in the pond require some type of liner to keep the water from seeping into the ground. This will also keep the edges of the pond from crumbling or sinking under the weight of plants or edging. Ponds, in particular, can be lined with a pre-molded liner, a flexible liner, or another type of material.

Here are some liner options to think about for your pond or water feature:

- Pre-molded liners come in different shapes, and some come with plant shelves built in to accommodate water gardening. Cheaper pre-formed liners are made of plastic, which can last about ten years. This life span can be shorter in a hotter climate, where the liner is exposed to sunlight consistently. More expensive pre-formed liners are made out of fiberglass, and these can have a longer life of more than ten years and, in some cases, up to 30. Although many shapes are available, some gardeners feel using this type of liner limits their creativity. Choosing this liner might be perfect for those who hope to do less design and creative work and get to a completed project sooner.

- If the entire point of you creating your pond is to express your creativity and make a one-of-a-kind yard setting, a flexible liner might be better for your purposes. Using a flexible liner allows you to create a pond of any shape, size, or depth.

Photo courtesy of Drs. Foster and Smith Aquatics

Flexible liner is sold as a small roll cut off a larger roll. The liner can then be unrolled, and the sheet of liner can be placed in a hole of any shape and trimmed to fit perfectly. The price of this type of liner varies based on the material of which it is made. Polyvinyl chloride (PVC) liners are cheaper and less resistant to sunlight, so they will wear out faster. Expect a PVC liner to last between five and ten years. Rubber liners are thicker. As it stands to reason, thicker liners will last longer. There are negative aspects to this type of liner. Flexible liner is more susceptible to damage than the pre-formed kind. Rocks or other sharp objects in the pond area can tear it.

- A more permanent pond can be constructed out of concrete. In most places, a permit will be required to dig and pour a concrete pool. Once the pond is dug, the excavated area might need reinforcing before the concrete is poured, due to the material's weight. The process will also take longer because the concrete has to be left to settle and dry. Then it might require covering with a layer of sealant to prevent lime or other minerals from leeching into the pond water. If you think a concrete pond is for you, this type of work, especially if it is intended to last for decades, might be left best to the professionals. If installed improperly, repairs can become costly and involved. A small amount of concrete or mortar can be mixed by a homeowner who has some experience with the medium according to the directions provided with purchase. This type of mixture can be used for small projects, such as stepping stones.

~~~~~~

Mixing Cement

The steps for mixing cement are as follows:

1. To mix cement for a footing or foundation, mix one part Portland cement, two parts sand, and three parts 1-inch gravel (called six-to-eights in quarries).

2. Add your water to the dry mix, not dry mix to water, and use a hoe to mix as you add the water. This is important because the dry mix tends to settle on the top of the mixing pan and becomes more difficult to mix.

3. Add your gravel to the water/cement mixture. Adding gravel will strengthen the mix for a more solid and stable foundation. The cement should be dry enough to hold peaks when you shovel it into the trench you have dug for the foundation, but wet enough to work with and level out when you place it.

If you have standing puddles of water on your cement mix after you shovel it into the trench, it is too wet and will leave air pockets as the cement cures and dries, which will cause it to be weak. There should be no air pockets in the cement, and if there are, work them out with the hoe until there are no puddles on the top of the mix. You must clean your tools before the cement hardens on them, or you will have a hard time chipping it off. To clean cement from your tools or from other surfaces, it is important to wash down the tools and surfaces with water after you have finished using them. Some cement can be removed from flat surfaces, such as brick, with a wire brush, but it is recommended that you prevent the cement from hardening where it is not wanted rather than try and clean it off after it has set. Once cement sets and hardens on tools, such as hoes and shovels, it is impossible to get it all off, and the tools are ruined.

- It is possible to create an aboveground pond or waterfall using concrete or pre-made backyard ponds sold at gardening or home improvement stores. These containers can be glass, which would resemble a giant aquarium, concrete, or cement with tiles on the inside to accent the pool. Garden supply stores and even local home improvement stores sell these containers. When shopping for one of these, inquire about delivery costs or have a plan for how you will transport the container home. Also, plan what you will do to protect the container in any extreme weather you might encounter in your area.

Once the site for your pond is excavated, underlayment will need to be placed before the liner to provide stability for the liner. Underlayment is filler material that gets placed between the liner and the earth. There is specific

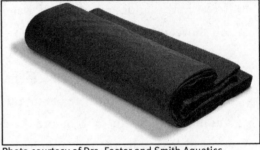

Photo courtesy of Drs. Foster and Smith Aquatics

underlayment material available through water gardening supply stores. It is similar to the padding you would place under your carpet in your home. This is the best choice because it is specifically designed for this purpose. If you cannot find underlayment material to buy or wish to go with a cheaper alternative, underlayment can be old carpet, shredded newspaper, or a shallow layer of sand, evenly packed.

Pond math

Once you have decided on the size of your pond, there are calculations you will need to make to purchase your pieces of equipment.

Volume: The volume of your pond is calculated using its length, depth, and width. Your pond's capacity is a measurement you will likely need to purchase a pump. To find your pond's volume in gallons, multiply the length by the width by the depth by 7.5. Each cubic foot holds 7.5 gallons of water.

Length _____ feet × width _____ feet × depth
_____ feet × 7.5 = pond volume _____ gallons

If your pool is 10 feet long and 5 feet wide, with a depth of 5 feet:

$$10 \times 5 \times 5 \times 7.5 = 1875$$

Surface area: Why is it important to know the surface area of your pond? You might not need this measurement when shopping for equipment, but you will need to know and think about what it means, especially if you hope to keep fish. The pond's surface area is the surface of the pond you can see. This is important because the surface receives the sunlight and provides heating for the pond. If your pond is a square, you multiply the height by the width to get the surface area. To get an approximate measurement of the surface area of an irregularly shaped pond, imagine your pond within a square, then multiply the height of that square by the width.

For example, if your pond is about 5 feet deep and 3 feet wide, your surface area is 15 feet.

Filters

Next, a filter might be needed depending on the use you have in mind for your pond. A pond that will only contain water and plant life should be able to balance out its own bacteria. Such a pond, when stocked properly and well taken care of, will not need a filter. A pond that has a waterfall or fountain powered by a pump will also need a filter to work in conjunction with the pump.

If you intend to stock your pond with fish, you will need a filter to keep the water clean. Although fish will balance their own environment in a small aquarium or pond, they cannot keep a large pond clean. They need some kind of help to balance out the environment. Having fish in your pond with no filter is like having the Brady Bunch in your house with no Alice to clean up after them.

As with the supplies needed for your pond, there are also different types of filters available:

- Mechanical filters are the more conventional filters you might have seen. They begin working and cleaning right away by capturing particles of fish food, waste, or plants. Those purchasing a submersible pump to power a fountain or waterfall might get a mechanical filter attached to the pump unit, which will do the job fine for a small- to medium-sized pond. A large-sized pump will work better with a separate filter unit. Most mechanical filters will require cleaning about once a week.

• Biological filters are another choice for those keeping a fish pond. They convert the fish wastes in the water, which can put your pond's chemicals out of balance, into harmless substances. This type of filter works more slowly but only requires cleaning about once a month. *Biological filters will be discussed further in Chapter 9.*

If you are using a biological filter, you might choose to use an ultraviolet (UV) clarifier in conjunction with the filter. This might also be an item to add down the road if you find that the pond has an algae problem. In this clarifier, an ultraviolet bulb is used to kill the cells of algae and certain aquatic bacteria and parasites. Many pond owners choose to use this in conjunction with the biological filter because the biological filter works slowly while the clarifier gives faster results.

Pond skimmer

Photo courtesy of Drs. Foster and Smith Aquatics

Another piece of equipment that might not be necessary depending on your application is a pond skimmer. A skimmer is a different form of mechanical filter, one that traps dirt and debris inside a bag, which you can change out as needed. The frequency of bag changes can vary depending on the nature of your yard, but it is most likely once a month in times of heavy debris and less frequently at other times of the year.

If you have a smaller budget to start with, pass on the skimmer. A skimmer is more of an add-on item because it is not strictly necessary for the operation of the pond. You might choose to wait until the first year of your pond's life to add this item. Spend the first year observing how much time you spend cleaning debris out of the pond, especially in the times of the year when leaves and pollen are strewn about the yard. Does the amount of time you spend offset the added expense of a pond skimmer?

If you have decided to spend the money on this, look for a high-quality pool skimmer that will last you a long time. The skimmer should have a sturdy metal frame that will not rust quickly. For homeowners trying to entice small animals to the pond, look for a skimmer with a brush panel, which will collect inert debris, such as leaves and debris, but will not allow fish and frogs to be collected.

Plants or pumps?

Pond air pumps are unnecessary for every pond. Air pumps are marketed as a tool to bring oxygen-depleted water to the surface and aerate the pond. Adding air to the pond or lake is necessary, especially if you have a large-sized pond. Certain fish and plants will gasp up all the air in the water, and more oxygen will need to be injected into the water for them to survive. This can be achieved by adding oxygenating plants to the pond area.

Oxygenating plants, such as hornwort or waterweed, will grow rapidly and will require regular trimming so they do not spread too fast. Despite this rapid growth, oxygenating plants will not work as quickly as an air pump. When using plants to aerate the water, you might have to tolerate short periods during which the water is cloudy, murky, or discolored with a brown or green tinge. If you are keeping certain fish in your pond, such as koi, they might require more air than the pond naturally contains.

In the wintertime, once the pond is frozen, the oxygen level in the pond will go down. Similarly, in the summertime, the oxygen level will decrease because warmer water does not hold oxygen as well as cooler water. This can be a matter of life or death for your fish, which need oxygen to digest and process food.

Air pumps are also used as a solution for an overabundance of algae. If you hope to add more air to your pond through a mechanism, consider the elements you want to add before purchasing a separate air pump. A water feature, such as a waterfall or fountain, will also oxygenate the water as the water splashes into the pond. Depending on the volume of water your feature's pump moves, you might find this oxygenation sufficient.

If you are planning on installing a fountain or waterfall, it will likely need a pump to supply the pressure behind the flowing or spraying water. Pumps are available in varying sizes and types, depending on the volume of your pond and how fast you want to move the water:

Stainless Steel Submersible Water Feature Pump. Photo courtesy of Drs. Foster and Smith Aquatics

- Submersible pumps are pumps that sit inside the body of water they pump. The sound that results can be more muffled than external pumps and quieter for pond-side visitors seeking peace. These are the cheaper type of pump. Submersible pumps come in different sizes. To find out what size pump you need, calculate the capacity or the head height of the fountain. When in doubt, it is better to purchase a pump with a larger capacity because you can find a way to cut back on the water supply to the pump if you want less, but there is no way to make a small pump go bigger.

- External pumps sit entirely outside the water and are used for large-sized water features. Similar to the pumps used for swimming pools, they can be too noisy and costly for most backyard ponds. This type of pump will require its own protection from the elements, so you will have to consider this in your design.

External pump. Photo courtesy of Drs. Foster and Smith Aquatics

Statues or fountainheads

A fountain also will require its crowning glory: a statue from which the water flows out or a fountainhead, a piece that attaches to the water hose and creates the spray. You also can choose to create a wall fountain, a fountain with a wall from where the water flows, out of a statue's head in the wall.

Here are fountain options:

- Statuary fountains are sold at garden or home improvement stores, complete with installation instructions. Some of these will come with a filter and pump included while others will require you to purchase and install the pump separately. Be sure to understand exactly what pieces come with the statuary you are purchasing.

- Spray fountains require a nozzle or fountainhead to create the spray pattern. This is a variation on the classic design: a pipe or length of tubing connected to a nozzle that sprays the water into the  air. Spray fountains also can be purchased at garden or home improvement stores.

Electricity

You might need certain electrical elements to operate the water feature. The pump, filter, and any lights you want to add will require power. Supplying power to the pond might seem intimidating, particularly for those who have no experience working with electrical equipment.

Here are the different electric components you might need to go with your pond:

- A 120-volt system is the standard size used for outdoor electricity. This is a more complicated application that might require a permit or professional help. Low voltage systems are also available. These systems convert the power they receive from your home's power supply into a less powerful current. This is enough power to operate a small feature, yet not enough to electrocute anyone.

- A power cable will run from the circuit breaker to the equipment. This power cable is best installed underground because the splash or runoff from the feature or rainwater can electrify or damage it. If you are using a 120-volt system, it is unnecessary to bury the cable. It can be hidden in foliage or under rocks placed directly on the surface.

- Next, you will need to install an outlet into which you will plug the equipment. A ground fault circuit interrupter or GFCI outlet is a good idea for the outlet. If you live in a newer home, it is likely that these are the same outlets you have in your home. They have two buttons between the actual outlet holes: one marked "test" and the other "reset." This type of outlet will cut off the power if necessary because it can sense an electrical overload. If somehow water were to come into contact with it, the outlet would stop the electrical current. You can then restore power to the outlet by pressing the reset button.

GFCI Outlet

- Electrical add-ons, such as pond lights, are best if they are intended for this purpose. Underwater lights are specially constructed for constant exposure to water. Specialty garden stores and pond equipment retailers have lights intended for underwater use. From LED bullet lights to large diameter halogen spotlights, different sizes and shapes are available to create any effect you might desire. Consider using multiple spotlights pointed toward the fountain or waterfall from different spots within the pool. This can be complemented with lights placed pond side or in the bushes around the pond. These types of lights, suitable for outdoor use, can be purchased at any large retailer or home improvement store.

Equipment in a box

Online specialty retailers abound, and they offer kits for every kind of water feature imaginable. Even pre-formed liners are sold in a box. They are rolled up into a box and unrolled and unsnapped on arrival to you. These liners are made of a form of polyethylene and guaranteed for 10 to 20 years. These kits provide a good value for the price. The equipment includes standard-quality equipment, and all the parts are made to fit together, which makes installation easy.

Determining Your Budget

With an idea of what supplies you will need to purchase, you can begin estimating your budget. Any homeowner who has attempted a renovation or remodel of some sort knows that sticking to a particular budget is a more difficult task than it seems. Planning well and taking the time to comparison shop for supplies will help you make sure you get the best prices. Be sure of exactly what parts you intend to buy before you start shopping, and do not be swayed by sales clerks or online advice from retailers trying to sell you extra things you do not need.

No budget can account for the unexpected expenses, impulse buys, and extra items you will decide to purchase. Get the anticipated measurements of your finished pond so you can accurately predict how much you will need to spend on liner, underlayment, and edging materials.

Budget worksheet

To determine an approximate cost of your project before you begin, itemize the amount you anticipate spending or have already spent on the following items:

Liner	
• *Pre-formed Liner-fixed cost*	$
• *Flexible Liner-anticipated amount needed × cost per foot*	$
Underlayment	
• *Newspaper, carpet, sand, or underlayment material*	$
Stones/Edging Material	
• *Rocks or Pebbles*	$
• *Logs*	$
• *Bricks*	$
Filter	$
Pump	$
Fountainhead	
• *Statuary*	$
• *Spray fountainhead*	$
Plants	
• *Amount of plants needed × average cost of plants*	$
Fish	
• *Amount of fish needed*	$
• *Fish food*	
Labor costs	
• *Total professional services rendered*	$

Types of services:

CHAPTER 3

Backyard Ponds

Making the decision to add a pond to your backyard is the first in a line of decisions you will have to make about your water feature. It might seem overwhelming, especially once you start shopping for supplies. Different choices exist in almost every type of pond supply and each promises to be the best choice. Get familiar with the different types of equipment available by looking online. Choosing the right liner for your project is important to match the life of the pond with your expectations. Or, you might choose to skip the liner and go with concrete. There are also large containers available to create a large aboveground pond, if you prefer this look.

Basic Shapes and Sizes of Backyard Ponds

The shape of your ponds and the liner you choose are interrelated. If you want to create a shape of your own that is customized to your yard, you will most likely need to use flexible liner. If you have chosen one of the more popular shapes, you have the option of using a pre-formed liner. Alternately, it might be possible to order a custom-made, pre-formed liner in whatever shape you desire. The next sections will explain the differences between the two.

Customized shapes

Flexible pond liner being installed.
Photo courtesy of Douglas Brown.

For best results with a customized, one-of-a-kind shape, first consider flexible liner. Flexible liner is a long section of material that can be placed in any shape with cutting and folding. Flexible liner, as the name suggests, lends itself to many applications for the creative.

From a practicality standpoint, flexible liner might be easier to transport home in your vehicle. If you purchase a small amount of flexible liner, they might give it to you as a folded sheet. Or, for a larger amount, you might get a small roll. Flexible liner comes at different prices, and the material will vary based on the price. Cheaper liner is a type of plastic, likely polyvinyl chloride (PVC), which will be more cost effective but will not last as long as rubber.

Man made rubber, such as ethylene propylene diene monomer (EPDM), is the more expensive option. EPDM is thicker than plastic and is expected to last longer. Some flexible EPDM liners are warrantied from the manufacturer for as long as 20 years. This warranty does not cover tears or damage done by your installation. Most of these warranties only cover damage due to sun exposure and manufacturer defect. This can be easier to bring home than a pre-molded liner.

Pond liner is black, or a dark color, so it is not readily visible to pond visitors. If there is a downside, it is the life expectancy. Flexible liner is known to deteriorate over time. This deterioration will get worse with exposure to sunlight, so those who live in sunnier climates will find the life of the liner might be a few years shorter than indicated by the manufacturer. The ultraviolet rays will permeate the liner over time, and as it wears, it will become more susceptible to tears and leaks. There is also a chance it will snag or rip on rocks or sharp edges. If there are trees or any other strong-rooted plants too close to a pond with flexible liner, they can also pierce through and create a leak. Many people purchase their pond supplies online. Purchasing a pre-formed liner online is a solution to the transportation problem, but you run the risk of getting a liner that does not look the same as it did online. Buying flexible liner online, especially one with a good brand name and a warranty, is safe. As with any online shopping, be sure to check the return policy of the website from which you purchase it, in case you receive something you were not expecting.

Purchasing flexible liner

Calculating how much flexible liner you need begins with good measurements. Figure out the width, depth, and length of the pond conclusively. If you are using a free-form shape you have created from your own design, you will have to do estimating. It might help to imagine the shape contained inside a rectangle. Add the anticipated pond width to twice the anticipated depth. Add 2 feet to this number to create extra liner, just in case your pond ends up being slightly deeper or wider after the excavation than you figured. Next, take the pond's length and add it to twice the depth, then add 2 feet to that figure.

Width of pond _____ feet + (pond depth _____ feet × 2) + 2 feet = width of liner needed

Length of pond _____ feet + (pond depth _____ feet × 2) + 2 feet = length of liner needed

If your pond is 4 feet deep, 4 feet wide, and 6 feet long:

Width of pond 4 feet + (pond depth 4 feet × 2) + 2 feet = width of liner needed

4 + 8 + 2 = 14 feet

Length of pond 6 feet + (pond depth 4 feet × 2) + 2 feet = length of liner needed

6 + 8 + 2 = 16 feet

When in doubt, add extra footage to the amount of liner you are purchasing. It is better to have too much liner than too little because adding more liner and creating a seam is complicated and can get messy. Any extra liner you cut off can be reused for other projects, such as small container ponds or skinny streams.

~~~~~~

Pre-made shapes

Pre-formed liners are liners already fabricated in a shape, made out of plastic or fiberglass. They look somewhat similar to a kiddie pool, only deeper and much sturdier. If you purchase a pre-formed liner from a local retailer, you will have to find a way to bring it home or have it delivered. Purchasing online is a good way around this problem because many websites offer free shipping. Some pre-formed liners come with built-in shelves for plants at pre-designated heights. When shopping for a pre-formed liner, bring a tape measure so you can measure how far down the plant shelves are. Then, research the best height for the plants you plan to use. Manufacturers place these shelves at popular heights, but that does not necessarily mean they will be the right height for your application. If you are planning a natural-looking, spill waterfall, some liners come with a lip designed to help create a waterfall drop. Pre-formed liners are expected to last about 10 years or more, depending on the material of which they are composed. Convention wisdom is that the life of a pre-formed liner pond is longer than the flexible liner. However, it can depend on the material used. Check if your liner is warrantied against damage and for how long.

Popular shapes of pre-formed liners

Different shapes of pre-formed liner exist, but these are the most popular:

- Basic Geometric Shapes: Simple shapes, such as circles, squares, or rectangles, are easily found in a pre-formed liner. Even triangle pools that can slot into a corner of the yard are available. These shapes have a more formal and less natural look but lend themselves to diverse designs. Consider using one of these shapes and applying different edging or a different type of fountain to make it your style. A rectangle pond, framed by a raised edge of cool blue tiles, can be the focal point of a Mediterranean-inspired backyard oasis. The same rectangle, edged in concrete with a softly trickling statuary, can anchor a tribute to French or Italian style.

- Kidney Shaped: One of the most frequently seen shapes for a pond, the kidney shape allows the water in the pond to circulate and move. The lobes allow for movement of the water around the shapes. It is also easy to create a dramatic effect by positioning a waterfall or large planting along the rounded side of the pool.

Choosing a liner in a geometric shape does not rule out the possibility of a natural-looking pond. Smart design choices can transform a pond of any shape. Think about a grass edge to your pond instead of a raised edge, though you will have to remain vigilant about scooping out any grass clippings that fall in the pond before they can upset the pond water.

In this type of design, it is a good idea to install a concrete mowing strip under the edge. To do this, construct a ledge around the edge of the pond when excavating the site. *For more information on how to excavate the site, refer to the Constructing a Pond section later in this chapter.* Next, use mortar or concrete to reinforce the area, beginning at the ledge and stretching up to just under the surface, where you can cover it with a thin layer of sod.

You can place plants with tall, leafy stalks just inside the pond to give the look of a reedy marsh. Or, consider adding a bog garden along one side. As the bog fills out and the plants begin to grow and bloom, the shape will look less like a perfect figure and more like a softly edged natural pond. Large slabs of natural stone, such as limestone, around the edge of the pond will fool the eye into thinking the shape of the pond is not as perfect as it is. Creating a rock outcropping from one edge of the pond can also soften the corners, which would make the shape look less harsh and rigid.

Designs to avoid

Although you can make a pond any shape you choose, certain design elements will make it more difficult to create and maintain. It is best to avoid a design that has too many "fingers," or lobes of water, that draw away from the main pool of water. A design that has little circles or lobes of water on each end will be harder to create, line, and fill. The pond water will not circulate well through these segments. The water that does get trapped in these portions will be colder than the rest, and you will find it hard to maintain a stable water condition if the pond temperature is not consistent. If you have fish, the dip in temperature between areas might upset them.

Deciding on depth

Deciding on the depth for your pool is another area where you can let your creativity be your guide. For practical purposes, a simple viewing pond should be about 12 inches deep. This is deep enough to enjoy the pond without having it look like an undersized ditch. Even if you are not starting out with plants and fish, if you think you might want to add them later, your pond will need to be deep enough to accommodate them. Ponds that will become water gardens need to be deeper, at least 18 inches, to allow the plants optimal conditions.

A habitat for fish needs to be at least 24 inches, but this depends on the type of fish intended to stock the pond. Some species will demand a minimum depth of a few feet. Consider your local climate as well. Those who live in a more moderate climate can dig a deeper pond with the hope of keeping the fish in the water throughout winter. But someone who lives in a cold climate might not want to dig such a deep pond because it will require draining and dismantling equipment each winter.

A fountain will function better if it has a certain depth to it. Although there are small fountains available for smaller ponds, if you hope to create a fountain, your pond should ideally be at least a few feet deep.

You can slope the bottom of your pond to a deeper depth in the middle if you would like. Using a flexible liner, this might be harder to install, but it will create a multipurpose pool. A pre-formed liner might already do this for you by coming with plant shelves of different heights built in.

When in doubt, dig the pond deeper. It is almost impossible to make the pond deeper after it has already been installed. To do so, you will have to undertake a project as large as the initial pond installation. Draining the pond, digging a larger hole, and reinstalling the old liner or installing a new one will not seem worth the few more feet it will net you. Rather than put yourself through this type of large-scale backyard renovation twice, consider adding a few extra feet from inception. The size that seems too large to you at the inception of your pond will seem much smaller once it is dug.

Oversized ponds

If you are building an extremely large pond with flexible liner, you might not be able to find a liner wide enough. In this case, you might have to seam two pieces of liner together. You have options to facilitate this. Pond specialty stores carry sealant and tape for flexible liner. The tape comes on a roll similar to duct tape, but it is waterproof and can be used underwater. Look for good quality sealant tape meant for this specific purpose. Sealant comes in a tube, and it is waterproof and safe for underwater use. However, it might be more difficult to apply and can be messy.

Edging and Extras

The finishing touches are what take your pond from an amateur-looking hole in the yard to a beautiful new addition to the garden. Landscaping and added extras around the edges of your pond will serve an aesthetic and functional purpose. Although it might seem to be something that can wait until after the pond is created, it is better to choose early on.

Edging

Purchasing the edging in advance is also advisable. Depending on the form of edging you choose, it can most likely help you even as you create the pond. Edging that has some weight to it, such as rocks or logs, can be used to secure the edges of the flexible liner after you have cut it to size to make the filling of the pond easier.

Flat stone was used around the edges of this pond.

Different types of stone are available to go around the pond, depending on the purpose you have in mind. Flat stones around the edges can provide a stable edge. Paver stones are a type of stone used on walkways or patios. Pavers are made of concrete or a natural stone, such as sandstone. These make a good, flat, even surfaces for stepping on. They can also help you create a lip, which will discourage rainwater and yard runoff from entering the pond if the yard has a slope. It will prevent stray lawn clippings from falling into the pond where they will upset the water balance. Pavers are a popular choice because they are affordable and come in many sizes.

Gardeners with the know-how can use brick to create a raised edge to the pond. This gives a more formal and professional look, but it requires knowledge of brickwork. Although laying a few rows of brick is not difficult, trying to complete any new process for the first time is not advisable while you are in the middle of a large project. Delays will hold up the completion of the project and lead to frustration.

Large rocks or small stones lend a more natural look than a flat stone. Limestone slabs give a natural look in a neutral color. They also help balance the pond water's quality, thanks to their alkaline chemistry. Smaller stones, such as gravel, cobbles, or pebbles, can create a beach along one side of a pool for a wildlife viewing. You also can choose to intersperse small stones between plants along the edge of the pond.

Photo courtesy of Douglas Brown.

If you will be placing a pebble beach, consider adding something to stop the pebbles from falling in and collecting on the bottom of your pond. This can be as simple as a row of larger stones or brick placed just under the water's edge where the pebbles stop. Gravel might be available in different blends and colors to accent your design. If you live near a beach, you can collect small shells to wash and place along your beach. This will lend a more authentic, local look to your pond.

Logs or wooden edging should be pretreated because constant exposure to water and sunshine will cause it to wear and bleach. Look for a wood preservative that is safe for this purpose and not just meant to protect wood from occasional rainwater exposure. Whatever finish you use to coat the wood, ensure it is safe for fish and will not leech any substances into your pool.

Reinforcing the edges

If the edging you are using is heavy, such as large boulders or heavy limestone slabs, you might be concerned about weight. You have some options: You can reinforce the edging somehow, or you can pre-plan and create a designated shelf for this purpose. While excavating the pond, dig a shelf around the outer rim of the pond wide enough on which to set the edging. Cover this shelf with flexible liner, the same as the rest of the pond. If you are using a pre-formed liner, this approach might not work as well because the pre-dug earth shelf without liner risks erosion from the water.

You can choose to reinforce the edges using mortar or concrete. If you anticipate having foot traffic from visitors, this will provide peace of mind for you as a homeowner. It also might add to the value of your home for resale because potential buyers will appreciate the extra expense and quality. You can reinforce the edges with a concrete or brick strip. Simply dig a ledge when excavating the hole. Then fill that strip with concrete or two bricks mortared together. You can then mortar the edging to this strip or lay a row of topsoil before setting the edging on it.

Skip across the pond

Stepping stones are the closest people come to walking on water, so it is no wonder they cannot resist them. If you have younger children, stepping stones will be more appealing to them, so it might be better to wait until they grow older to add them. Stepping stones can be purchased pre-made, as large boulders with a flattened top for walking on, or you can construct your own. If you are building a smaller, shallower pond, it might be possible to simply add small pavers or stepping stones as a pond crossing.

If your pond is deeper, you can attach pre-made flat stepping stones to concrete blocks or a brick pillar using concrete or mortar. This will make them usable for walking across the pool. For the stones to support the weight that will be on them without destroying the liner, they will need to be reinforced. This is done by adding a concrete pad under the underlayment during the process of building the pond. Therefore, they will have to be part of the initial plan and design of the pond, or the pond will have to be drained and dug up to add them in a manner that is safe. Stay alert after installing the stones. Clean them to keep them from creating buildup, and walk on them to make sure they are stable.

Photo courtesy of Drs. Foster and Smith Aquatics.

Constructing a small footbridge that spans a portion of a larger pond is an option for gardeners who are handy with a hammer. A bridge adds a certain whimsy to a backyard garden, but consider how much room you have before beginning. A bridge jammed into a small space can look out of place and forced.

Family Activity: Edging the Pond

If you have older children who are eager to help with the pond, designing an edge to the pond can be a fun weekend project to complete after your pond has been dug. Helping you to create a new part of the pond can help sustain the initial excitement your children have developed around the pond.

A popular way to give flash to the edge of your pond is to use silicone caulk to place a decorative element around the edge of the pond. Depending on how picky you are about the colors and design, you might want to allow them to choose the edging. You can take the children to a craft store to help you select something inexpensive, such as small glass stones, shells, or mosaic tiles. They can help you draw and lay out a pattern in which you will apply them. Then you can use the caulk to set them in place.

Decorative rocks or stepping stones are another fun way to involve your children. To make your own decorative stepping stone, you will need:

- A cement mold. You can substitute a baking pan if you do not have a mold.

- A small amount of cement. *For instructions on how to mix cement, see Chapter 2.*
- Decorative elements, such as small stones, shells, or tiles.

First, plan the design of the stepping stones. If you plan to create mosaics, you will need to break the tiles. You can tap them with a hammer through a towel. The children can write messages with their fingers or place their handprints in the wet cement. Or, they can place the stones and shells in the cement to make a design.

Once the designs are ready, mix the cement and pour it into the mold. Even the cement out so it is flat at the top. The children now have 20-25 minutes to create in the wet cement. Let the stepping stones dry for a few days, then remove them from the mold, spray them with water, and wrap them with plastic wrap. Continue this process for the next week.

If you have created a mosaic design, you will need to add some grout to the tiles. Apply grout with a special tool intended for this purpose and let it dry.

Constructing a Pond

Creating a pond is not a complicated affair, but all the steps should be followed to avoid problems at a later stage. Completing the installation alone is not impossible, but enlisting help is a better idea. The physical part of the work, such as excavating the hole and moving the dirt out of the way, can eat up a large chunk of time with only one set of hands.

Whether you use flexible or pre-formed liner, you will find it helpful to have some helpers on hand. Although not particularly heavy, flexible liner is too large and awkward for one person to maneuver comfortably. To place the folds in the liner, it will be helpful to have the edges weighed down. A pre-formed liner is awkward to move and can be heavy if it is made out of fiberglass. Placing the liner inside the hole might take a few attempts, and you might have to lift and replace the liner several times. Having someone to backfill the pond hole with sand as you fill the liner with water will make the process faster. Also, having someone help you think of solutions to unforeseen problems as you create your pond can be valuable.

Consider inviting some friends and having a pond excavation party, or get your family involved. If all else fails, you might be able to hire some extra help at different stages of construction.

Step 1: Designate the area

The area that will be the pond cleared and ready for marking. Photo courtesy of Drs. Foster and Smith Aquatics.

Begin by marking the site for the pond. If you are using a flexible liner, you can trace around the area you have planned for your design with spray paint or chalk, or stake the area with rope and stakes. The rope and stakes might be the most time consuming, but they will provide a definite outline, whereas chalk might wear away during the excavation process. A garden hose also can be used to lay out the shape of the pond as long as it is not too complicated. If using a pre-formed liner, follow the same process to trace around the shape of the liner. The actual hole you dig will need to be slightly larger than the

The pond outline designated with spray paint. Photo courtesy of Drs. Foster and Smith Aquatics.

pre-formed liner itself, so the liner can be placed and the remaining space backfilled with sand or dirt.

Step 2: Excavation

The area of the pond excavated with the pond's varying depths in mind. Photo courtesy of Drs. Foster and Smith Aquatics.

After tracing the pond, you have to excavate the area. Refer back to the previous section to make sure your proposed depth is suitable for your intended purposes. If you are excavating by hand, you might find it easier to use a shovel for the middle area and a spade for the fine edge work. If you are renting equipment for this purpose, it will take time to learn to operate the equipment. Add extra time to your anticipated rental length to compensate.

A waterfall box strategically placed within a hole dug at the top of the pond's slope. Photo courtesy of Drs. Foster and Smith Aquatics.

After digging, make sure the edges of your pond are level. If you are planning to create built-in shelves for edging or plants, dig a shelf around the outer rim of the pond wide enough on which to set the edging. Plant shelves can be anywhere from 10 to 15 inches under the waterline. If you dig plant shelves, make sure they are level with one other. If you plan to add a heavy statuary or large underwater stepping stones, you will need to dig an extra hole for a concrete pad.

Step 3: Placing the liner

After the excavation, your next step will vary based on what kind of liner you are using.

If you are using a pre-formed liner, you will then place a small layer of dirt or sand in the hole (you would not use underlayment for this type of installation) before putting the liner

Photo courtesy of Drs. Foster and Smith Aquatics.

in the excavated hole. Fill the liner with water slowly, and place more dirt or sand around the liner as it fills.

If you are using a flexible liner, begin by placing the underlayment in the excavated hole. Then place the liner on top of the underlayment in the excavated hole. Fold the liner where needed to make the sheet fit to the shape of the hole. This might take several tries to find the right placement, so be prepared to spend time positioning the liner. Do not rush this step because the liner needs to be placed as well as possible with the entire excavated surface covered. Patience and attention to detail will pay off in the long term. Smaller folds in the liner will be less visible than larger ones.

Step 4: Filling the hole

When filling the hole, you might need friends to hold the liner in place. Alternately, you can place something to weigh the edges down and keep them in place. Fill the pond with hose water slowly so the bottom of the liner can settle and mold to the excavated area.

The finished pond and waterfall. Photo courtesy of Drs. Foster and Smith Aquatics

The pond liner held in place by natural-looking rocks and stones. Photo courtesy of Drs. Foster and Smith Aquatics

CASE STUDY: FEEL THE RELAXATION

Robert Hawe
General Manager
Acurel®/Loving Pets
www.acurel.com
www.lovingpetsproducts.com

I have 20 years of experience as a retail store owner selling garden ponds and fish. You learn something new every day. It is relaxing and enjoying for me, and I want others to feel the relaxation that I receive from a pond. Keeping up with pond advice from forums and blogs can be helpful. Every township or city has different regulations, so check with your local township or city's website.

I do not have a pond; however I did install a 12,000-gallon koi pond for my neighbor that I maintain and enjoy on a daily basis. The pond keeps getting bigger with more features added on every time you sit by it. After we installed the 12,000-gallon pond, we installed about 1,000 feet of LGB outdoor railroad to go around the pond, with a bridge going over the pond. The combination of trains and fish is a dream of every 41-(me) and 80-(my neighbor) year-old little boy. The only negative is that we have a short season and have to close the pond down in late September. But this will depend on each regional area. I do not see any drawbacks, only environmental biodiversity.

Design whatever gives you the most enjoyment in your yard or space. The bigger the better. Do not be scared. There are people who will help and guide you along the way.

Plants

Photo courtesy of Douglas Brown

For those not ready to tackle water gardening, plants can be placed in planters around the edge of the pond or planted in the ground around the pond. A formal-looking pond can be trimmed with well-kept hedges or rosebushes. If you are striving for a more natural look, this can be achieved by placing plants in the pond. The stalks and flowers will emerge from the waterline over time. *For a more detailed overview of water gardening, turn to Chapter 6.*

When choosing plants for your pond, consider what they like. Plants, like any other living creature, have a natural preference about where they live. Certain plants, called marginals, will flourish at the edges of the pond near the pond's bank. Others, called submersible plants, prefer to be completely submerged in the water. Floating plants do best unrestrained by any kind of pot when on the water's surface. Those plants that prefer to be in the soft soil of a bog are called bog plants.

Placing marginal and submersible plants

To place the plants within the pond, there are methods you can use. Many pre-formed liners come with plant shelves built into them, on which you can sit a potted or basketed plant. If you are forming the pond yourself, you can build pond shelves into the pond's design. The excavated dirt from the site can be used to form shelves you can then cover with liner. This might be difficult if you are installing a pond for the first time. You might need some help from friends to lay the liner properly across this type of plant shelf.

Plant islands

Plant islands help a pond look natural. The added foliage reaching out of the middle of the water reminds the viewer of a natural landscape. Plant islands do not have to be difficult to construct. You can plan them into your design and mold them out of the excavated dirt as you shape your pond. For a simpler approach, you can place plants in planting baskets on top of those shelves, then place stones around the basket to hold it in place. Alternately, you can create a brick pillar to place plants on, similar to the way you can place stepping stones on a pillar.

Plant baskets

Floating plant basket. Photo courtesy of Drs. Foster and Smith Aquatics

Pond plants are rooty and will grow as far as you allow them, which can create chaos in your pond. For this reason, people choose to enclose the plants in planting baskets, the water equivalent to garden pots. This also will allow the plants to get the soil they need without creating a mess on the bottom of your pond or in your filter. After all, why do all that work with the liner just to end up with soil in your pond? There are also pots suitable for using in a submersible fashion if you prefer them to baskets. Planting baskets are made of dark plastic, in a netted-style mesh that blends well into the look of the pond. Planting baskets, by their nature, make it easier to see when the time is approaching for the plants to be trimmed or replanted. Loose soil also will upset the balance of the pond water. Keeping the plants in baskets allows you to remove them or change their location easily.

Preparing the plants to be introduced in the pool is a simple process:

Step 1: The basket will need to be lined to prevent soil from seeping into the pond area. This can be done with a square of permeable fabric, such as cheesecloth or burlap.

Step 2: Soil will need to be placed in the basket. Pack the soil down so it does not float away as soon as it is placed in the pool.

Step 3: Place the plant in the basket. Fill the basket with soil. On top of the soil, a small layer of rocks or gravel will help to keep the soil down.

Step 4: Put the plant in the water. If you are placing the plant on a shelf under the water's surface, keep in mind that only the top of the plants might break through the water at this point.

Floating plants

The plants you might have seen in ponds and want to include might be floating plants, which will not require planting. The added benefit of these plants lies in their ability to cover some of the pond's surface and provide shade and cover for fish. Beware, though, as some floating plants will spread uncontrollably. Some of these plants will be difficult, if not impossible, to remove.

Creating A Bog Pond

Attached bog garden in front of a house.

In the wilderness along the banks of a stream or river, you will find bogs, marshy, wet areas where certain plants flourish. A bog pond, also known as a wetland pond or a bog garden, is a shallow pond devoted to plants. It imitates a bog you would find in nature. If your hope is to keep a natural look, a bog attached to a water pond imitates the configuration seen in nature. However, the water between the two ponds should not mix much or it will upset the ecological balance.

A bog can be as shallow as 12 to 15 inches and serve its purpose fine. To encourage the plants to grow, the liner is filled with soggy soil. Compost from an existing heap can fill the liner just as well. Certain plants are best suited to a bog environment. Cattails will flourish in bog conditions but might overtake the pond if planted directly in the soil. In a warm climate, cannas will also enjoy being placed in a bog and will add color to the area. *More detail on these plants can be found in the appendix at the end of the book.*

A bog garden needs to have a natural look to be credible and realistic. Planting them around the edges of the pond in mesh baskets, the way you might in a pond, will not work as well because bog plants by nature like to be greedy and eat up space. They will grow and spread quickly if given the right amount of room. Instead, plant bog vegetation directly in the wet soil. Some of the plants best suited to a bog cannot tolerate being dry, so it is key for the soil to stay moist.

Over time, a bog will draw local wildlife to your yard. Snails and frogs will begin to migrate to enjoy the water.

Design Plan No. 2: A Bog Garden

Building an independent bog or wetland garden is similar to constructing a pond.

Adding a bog to your pond

1. If you choose to add a bog to the edge of a pond, begin by excavating the area. Even a small, shallow trough will suffice for a bog garden because they do not need to be deep. If you are installing the bog at the same time as the pond, you can use the same liner, as long as you place some kind of barrier between them. A small amount of pond water seeping back and forth between the ponds is alright, as long as it is minimal.

2. Next, lay a liner if you are using a different one than the pond's liner. Because this will be less taxing on the liner than a pond, you can use cheap PVC liner here.

3. Punch holes in the liner for irrigation.

4. Protect the area by adding a barrier between this area and your main pool area. This can be a high soil bank, rocks, or other form of edging.

5. Fill the trough with dirt or compost and plants.

Building a separate bog

Building an independent bog or wetland garden is similar to constructing a pond. You dig a hole and fill it with a liner.

1. Dig a hole at least 12 to 15 inches deep.

2. Fill the hole with a liner. Again, a bog does not need to be lined with heavy-duty liner the way a pond does. You can use a light, cheaper type of PVC.

3. Fill the liner with compost or soil. Make sure this material is soggy and does not get dry during the planting process.

4. Add a type of provision to keep the soil wet and soggy. You can continue to water the garden regularly on your own, or you can try one of the following ways:

   a) Insert a length of pipe with pre-drilled drainage holes directly into the bog pond soil vertically, with a few inches exposed from the earth. The water will enter through this end and enter the soil through the drainage hole. You can fix this by blocking the other end of the pipe before inserting it into the ground.

   b) More ambitious gardeners can use a longer-sized pipe, such as a horizontal pipe connected to a vertical pipe, to make one long L-shaped pipe. If you are unable to purchase such a pipe directly from a home improvement store, you can use an elbow connector to join two pipes on your own.

   c) Run a length of plastic pipe with drainage holes in it under the surface soil, midway deep in the pond. Again, leave a few inches sticking out of the surface in which to pour water.

These options will save you the added time of watering the area constantly and allow for an even distribution of water.

5. Certain plants are best suited to a bog environment. *More detail on these plants can be found in the appendix at the end of the book.* Plants in a bog garden do not get planted in baskets the way plants would be in a regular pond. These plants will get planted directly in the wet soil.

CHAPTER 4

Fountains

The movement of water through a fountain is fascinating to the human eye. Who has not spent time watching the water of a fountain burble up and spray, piercing the air with its flow? Or perhaps you prefer a statuary, designed to make you feel like you are taking your morning coffee at a trattoria in old world Italy? Here is an opportunity to jump and splash in the shallow pond around a fountain without getting arrested. The addition of a fountain to your backyard guarantees a new focal point. Whether a simple, burbling rock fountain or a large-scale wall fountain, guests will feel magnetized to the area.

Before adding a fountain, consider the effects on your water feature. If you have fish living in your pond, a small fountain will help circulate and aerate the water. However, too much displacement from a large fountain will upset the fish's environment. Similarly, the new water movement might upset floating plants, and you might see them move toward the edges of the pond to allow a wide berth.

The Simple Fountain

Perhaps because a fountain is such a thing of beauty, constructing one seems like it must be a difficult process. But the simplest type of fountain is not hard to create. A fountain only needs a pump, length of hose, and fountainhead to spray the water.

Different Types of Fountains

There are two basic types of fountains:

A geyser fountainhead. Photo courtesy of Drs. Foster and Smith Aquatics

- Spray fountains are fountains that spray water directly into the air. They are made up of a length of pipe connected to a spray nozzle or fountainhead. A pump circulates the water through this setup. The nozzle you choose for this type of fountain will dictate the pattern the water will spray in. There are different patterns traditionally used for fountains. A geyser is the most common, a straight column of water that shoots into the air. A bell is a shorter spray, with a rounder effect. Many of the fountainhead kits you can purchase will come with an assortment of nozzles that spray in different patterns. The nozzle will need to be dismantled and cleaned regularly to keep it spraying properly and cleanly.

Most spray fountains can be purchased in a kit, which will include the nozzle and fittings, a submersible pump, the electric cable, and a small pre-filter. The pre-filter cleans the water before it enters the pump. These kits will come with instructions and be easy to put together. When the pump is ready to be inserted in the pool, do not place it directly on the pond bottom. Debris and dirt are more likely to clog the pre-filter and eventually the pump if it sits there. Place the pond on a solid surface, such as a concrete pad or paver stone.

- Spill fountains are simpler by nature; they use gravity to aid in dropping the water along the water's intended course. The classic tap and basin design is an example of this. The water spills from the tap into the basin below, where tubing, connected to a pump, redirects the water back up to the tap. This same basic principle can be used to create a spill fountain with containers of your choosing. This type of fountain can be a ceramic vase with the vinyl tubing emerging

Tap and basin design fountain.

in the basin area. When the pump is on, the urn is filled, and it overflows softly into the pond beyond it. You can also stack containers or rocks to give the effect of water moving over steps. If any fountain lends itself to an informal style pool, it is the spill fountain, which can bubble softly out of a rock outcropping to suggest a natural spring. Or, a small container fountain in a simple ceramic urn or old-fashioned container can be added to the seating area near a natural-looking pond.

Things to know when installing a fountain

The fountain's head height is measured as the distance from the fountainhead nozzle to the water's surface. Fountain output is measured by head height, so knowing yours can be helpful.

Any kind of fountain will require a pump. There are two types of pumps available:

- Submersible pumps sit under the water's surface. They are easy to install and quieter than external pumps. For those concerned with conserving energy, a submersible pump is a greener choice.

- External pumps sit outside the body of water, like swimming pool pumps. They are more complicated and more suited to large-sized water features.

Although submersible pumps might seem to be the obvious choice, take time to consider your individual needs and situation. Each type of pump carries its own advantages and drawbacks. Submersible pumps might be easier to install, but if you have a grand water feature in mind, they might not provide the amount of power you need. An external pump will need some type of housing to protect it from the elements.

If you do not already know it, find your pond's volume. An easy way to do this is to note the amount of water it takes to fill the pond. You can use your water meter to track this as you fill the pond. Note the reading before and after filling the pond, then find out in what unit this meter measures. If it is in cubic feet, you are ready to go. Most meters, though, will not measure in feet but in gallons. This is easy to convert by multiplying the amount of gallons by 7.5. *If you are not able to measure water volume in this way, you can calculate it by using the equation back in Chapter 2.*

Select a pump that will displace half of your pond's total volume. When shopping, look for a pump that can move at least that much volume in an hour. To be safe, you can purchase a larger pump and turn it to a low setting.

As with much of the equipment needed for your pond, you can purchase all the fountain's components in a kit together or separately. If you purchase a kit, review which components are included and find out if installation instructions will be there.

Maximizing the effect of your fountain

To draw the viewer's eye, it is important for the focus to be the fountain's spray. Keep plants trimmed to a uniform height, at least a few inches below the fountain's peak. Use edging in a simpler finish and color so they blend into a uniform background for the fountain's spray. Submersible lights can be added at the base of the fountain, so a column of light shoots directly up with the water's spray.

Statuary Fountains

Statuary fountains are fountains that incorporate a statue figure or animal from which the water spills. These are seen in traditional designs. They are installed the same way as a spray fountain, with a length of pipe connecting to the statue. The statue is made of cement or concrete, and different figures can be found: animals spitting water out of their mouths, women tipping water out of vases, or even the classic Belgian boy peeing.

Watching your weight

If the statuary is over a certain weight, about 100 pounds or so, you might need to add a concrete reinforcement to keep it from sinking or damaging the pond. A concrete pad will need to be 4 to 5 inches thick and a few inches wider than the statues base. A pre-made concrete pad can be purchased from your local hardware store. Place the pad in the excavated area before the underlayment and liner. Depending on experience, you might be able to create this pad yourself, but it needs to be level. *See Chapter 2 for basic information on using concrete in your pond.* If your hand with the concrete is not steady, consider hiring a professional to construct the pad for you. The cost of such a small project should be minimal. The pad will raise the height of the statue accordingly. If raising the fountain will spoil the look of your feature, you might have to dig a hole for the pad.

CASE STUDY: TIPS FROM A MASTER GARDENER

Jill Chase & Bill Ticineto
New England
http://godogdign.com

Photo courtesy of Jill Chase

My husband and I have an interest in nature and gardening, so we researched water gardens and built one. I am a master gardener, and my husband builds beautiful arbors and pergolas for our gardens. We had made changes to our house that made our large driveway unnecessary, so we designed the frog pond and surrounding garden to take its place. We have a formal pool with a bronze fountain, water plants, and fish. The pond is 6-by-9 feet and surrounded by blue stone coping, and I have not thought it too small or too big for us. The fountain is a 2-foot frog leaping off a large lily pad to catch a dragonfly. It is situated near one end of the pond as if it is floating on the water.

Behind the "Frog King" is a bog area where overflow from the pond goes when we get rain (so the water level remains constant). This area is planted with large-leaved ligularia and grasses that hide the electrical and filter unit.

Photo courtesy of Jill Chase

I wanted a water garden, and when we found the vintage fountain at an antique show, we knew that was the start. The formal lines of the pond and garden are designed to be viewed from the windows above.

Photos courtesy of Jill Chase

After excavating as deep as we could (we had to drill through quite a bit of rock), we framed out the shape of the pool using railroad ties that we found on the property.

Photos courtesy of Jill Chase

We lined the bottom with sand, then pond liner. We installed inlets and outlets for a filtration system that hides in the plants behind the pond.

We have a kitchen garden, fruit trees, grape arbors, formal perennial beds, meadows, and a shade garden, and the water garden is the easiest to maintain with no weeding and no watering. Also, it is pretty, it has a soothing falling water sound, it reflects the light, and the fish and frogs always keep it interesting.

However, nature can be cruel, and the moment you start naming the koi, a heron comes along for a snack. Children love the fish and frogs it attracts. Be aware of that, and think about fencing and water depth to protect your fish. In the fall, I add a bio-lift product to the water to help break down organic matter that builds up over the winter, and I cover the pond with a net to prevent leaves going in. We live in New England, so we need to keep a small pump bubbling most of the winter to keep a hole in the ice for the fish.

I also over-winter any less hardy plants inside or in the basement. We clean and store the rest of the equipment for winter. In spring, we re-install. In summer, I add a small amount of dark dye made for ponds that helps shade the water, gives the fish cover from predators, and keeps algae from

Photo courtesy of Jill Chase

forming. With darker water, you notice the reflections on top and not the bottom. Keeping the right balance of fish to plants helps keep both happy. Once the plants get going in the summer, I do not run the filter because the plants filter the nutrients out of the water.

Wall Fountains

Wall fountains are a more complex project, but they can be seen as a type of statuary fountain because they are set up the same way: a length of pipe attaching to a statuary. This statuary is molded into a wall, for example, in the shape of an animal head spitting water or a spilling basin overflowing into another. Water spills out of the statuary and into a basin or the main body of the pool. The fountain can be built around an existing wall, or an ornamental wall created for this purpose can be installed.

Fountain mask.

If you are creating a new wall fountain, you will need a wall and a solid pool container to place it in. A wall sold for this purpose should have a fountainhead built into it. Then you will need the usual mechanical elements, such as a submersible pump and tubing to direct the water.

If you are choosing to build your wall fountain on an existing wall, you will begin with most of the same equipment. Instead of purchasing a wall with a built-in fountain, you would look for a fountain mask, available at home and garden stores. You can then do a direct installation, with the pump connecting to the tubing and the tubing emerging from the fountain mask. The mask then gets hung on the wall with the holding basin underneath it. The piping will need to be camouflaged in some way. Use your creativity to come up with a way to blend this tubing in. You can paint the tube if the wall is a dark color, or cover the exposed tube in nearby plants, if possible. The look can be less finished than a newly constructed wall fountain, but the amount of work required is less taxing.

Design Plan No. 3:
A Container Fountain

A container fountain can be constructed easily, especially if you already have completed the container pond project. Similar fountains sell at big box retailers for $20 or $30 each, but creating one of your own is more economical and will be customized to your taste and design. As with a simple container pond, just about any container can be used to create the pond. You can get creative based on the type of effect you want to create. A bamboo-inspired trickling fountain might look more at home in a ceramic urn, while a swiftly spinning wooden wheel fits better in a half barrel. Some vinyl tubing will move the water around, and a small submersible pump will power the fountain.

1. First, prepare the container and pump. Make sure the container is watertight and clean. For a smaller container, a liner might not be needed. Larger basins might need to be lined with PVC or plastic. Attach a piece of flexible vinyl or plastic tubing to the pump. Then, place the pump in the bottom of the container.

2. Put the other end of the tubing in the fountain. This can be:

   • A small statuary. Pre-formed concrete or cement statues come in all sizes.

   • A small slope constructed out of wood and rocks. A simple look is best in such a small space.

   • A piece of bamboo hollowed out or several pieces of bamboo positioned around the tubing.

- Stacked containers with a hole cut through the middle to create the illusion of steps of water.

- A grate with pebbles and stones resting on it.

3. Place any other decorative items, such as rocks, plants, or aquarium décor pieces, in the container.

4. Add water to the fountain, and once the fountain's pump is submerged, plug it in. The water should cover the pump, plus a couple more inches.

Design Plan No. 4: Shishi odoshi

An ancient Japanese fountain used to scare animals, a shishi odoshi is east to construct and looks fancy when displayed in a simple container. The actual "fountain" part consists of two bamboo pipes. The first pipe is suspended above the second and pours water into the bottom one to cause it to rock back and forth. The name shishi odoshi literally means deer scarer, and the simple fountain does serve a purpose. It will scare away some predatory birds, such as herons. Just as it repels the bird, its simple movement will draw your interest. Although it is meant to be placed outdoors in a garden,

Photo courtesy of Drs. Foster and Smith Aquatics

a small-scale shishi odoshi placed in a container pond looks sparsely elegant inside your office.

1. Select a body of water. This can be a container or an existing pond. A more traditional approach would be to place the shishi odoshi in a stone basin. If you choose to use a basin or container, scale the bamboo correctly, so the water falls where you want it to land.

2. Connect the submersible pump to the vinyl tubing. Place one end of the tubing in the hollowed bamboo pipe. This pipe should fit completely through the bamboo, so make sure the joints are hollow. Take another piece of hollowed bamboo and attach this to the main pipe by drilling a small hole through it and connecting the two using a small dowel.

3. To create the rocking part of the fountain, take the second bamboo pipe. Hollow this one three-quarters of the way, and cut the hollow end at an angle. Plug the other end so the pipe will hold water. Mount this piece below the first pipe so it will catch the water spilling from the first pipe.

4. Once both pipes are mounted and the fountain is filled, the bottom pipe should fill with water, tip over, and empty into the basin. To create the traditional sound, place a stone under the plugged end of the second pipe so the pipe strikes the stone as it tips and returns.

CHAPTER 5

Waterfalls

Still water can only be interesting for so long. The movement of water is what is fascinating. The ripple of the water and the way the waves crash against a beach — these are the things that captivate us. Waterfalls combine this movement with a sound of churning water, which along with the flecks of water on your face, combine to make an experience for all five senses.

There is no better example of water's might and majesty in nature than a waterfall. Waterfalls in nature, with their seemingly serene beauty and simultaneous power, draw attention. The way a quiet stream can burble into a whitewater rapid, and then down into a sheer drop, shows off nature's skill as an architect. In a smaller setting, such as a backyard water feature, the movement and sound of a waterfall make a focal point. It gives you an opportunity to show off your skill and finesse as a garden designer and turn your pond into something spectacular.

Once you have created a pond or fountain in the yard, the seemingly difficult task of creating a waterfall seems simpler. Most of the steps are similar. First is designing and planning the waterfall. Then is constructing the actual feature, by excavating, laying underlayment and a flexible liner, and placing edging. The next part is where it becomes a little different. You will fill the area with water and install the pump. Then you will have to place the plastic tubing to direct the water from the pond back up to the top of the waterfall. Then, to finish it up, test the pump and watercourse to make sure everything is flowing correctly before the installation is complete.

Slower moving waterfall that lightly trickles into the pond. Photo courtesy of Drs. Foster and Smith Aquatics

For those who want something that is more elaborate than a pond but that retains a natural feel, a waterfall is a smart choice. Keep in mind that a waterfall is not necessarily a loud, splashing distraction. A small dribble of water that slips between the rocks of an outcropping to land softly in the pond water is just as effective and something seen in nature. If you have a larger yard area with a natural slope to work with, a stream that leads to a waterfall is a beautiful way to incorporate water across a long area. If you are striving for a more contemporary look, a waterfall that creates more splash and displaces a larger volume of water, with concrete and metal construction, might be more appropriate.

The first waterfall

The oldest human-made waterfall, constructed by the Romans near Terni, in the Umbria region of Italy, still exists and welcomes tourists. Marmore Falls, or Cascata delle Marmore, as they call it in the native tongue, was engineered in 271 BC. The ancient Romans created the falls as a solution to a drainage problem. The fall is three separate drops in a meandering column, with a total height of 541 feet. These are still the tallest man made falls in the world. The falls split the water source with a power plant, and the water is turned on and off according to the needs of both elements. At pre-determined times, visitors can see the water being released through a gate and the falls surging from a low flow to its full roaring power.

Using the Slope of your Yard

In this example, a waterfall was added in the corner of a fairly level yard. The homeowners added rocks and plants to help it look more natural. Photo courtesy of Drs. Foster and Smith Aquatics

It is not necessary to have a natural slope to create a waterfall. The dirt you excavate from the pond site can be used for this purpose. If you intend to use the dirt to create a slope for the waterfall, you might want to use a wheelbarrow during excavation if you are excavating by hand. This will allow you to easily move the dirt from the pond area, off to a side area, until you are ready to place it for the waterfall. Keep in mind, though, that if you have a flat yard, you might not want to create too high of a slope because it will be difficult to make it look natural and at home in an informal yard. If you choose to build a high slope waterfall in a flat yard, the best way to make it look natural might be to surround it with plants and boulders, to make a larger area instead of just the waterfall. You could situate the waterfall in a corner of the yard to imitate a section of rock coming out of the corner, for example.

The natural slope of your yard is an area that can be used to advantage or disadvantage. It does not make sense to build an entire slope in a flat area of the yard if a natural slope exists. However, placing your body of water at the bottom of the slope can create the problems discussed earlier. Runoff, pesticides, clippings, and leaves are more likely to end up in your pond if it is situated in this area. These can be detrimental or even dangerous to your plants and fish. If you do situate your body of water at the bottom of a slope, test the water to stay on top of the state of the water. *Water testing will be discussed further in Chapter 6.*

As with ponds, a waterfall can be constructed using your own design; a slope you construct yourself out of dirt or the yard's natural slope; and flexible liner, a pump, and tubing. Or you can purchase a pre-formed waterfall. Pre-formed waterfalls can be made of fiberglass, cement, hard plastic or even stone. Many of these falls come with lights installed and come in designs to suit any formal or informal setup. If you have an existing pond and you hope to add a waterfall, a pre-formed waterfall is the easiest way to do so. Installation of this type of fall is simple. Many pre-formed waterfalls come with everything you will need, including the tubing and the pump. All you will have to do when you get it home is place it on the pond area and place the tubing so the water flows through the feature. If you have a local specialty store that sells these, they might even deliver and set it up for you.

If you need to construct your own slope, begin by placing the dirt evenly in the area where you will build. Try to place the dirt in a mound with even sides, and dig the watercourse along the appropriate side. Put boulders for support where they will fit in your design, but also where they will aid in keeping the mound together.

Waterfall Design

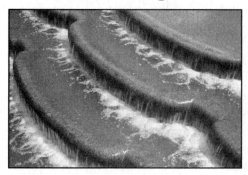

For those with a more formal design, a staircase style is an elegant and captivating idea. A stair-style waterfall imitates the look of a set of stairs by employing an actual staircase-shaped mold or a dirt staircase that you build in the excavation stage. The water moves quickly in this type of design and rushes over the steps to the bottom, creating a rushing sound and a visual of white tips churning over the feature. A bigger pond is required for this type of fall because a smaller pond might not have the volume of water needed unless it is relatively short with smaller steps. There also might be extra pieces required. For the water to flow properly across the steps, an extra piece, known as a waterfall box, might be needed. The waterfall box can be a deep square box, with a large, flat lip that comes out of one side. Waterfall boxes with a smaller capacity look similar to a large size dustpan. This piece will attach to the hose and collect water until there is enough to spill properly over the steps.

It is difficult, if not impossible, to achieve the kind of flow needed for this design with a simple length of tubing. If the look of a small flow of water snaking down the steps is the look you prefer, then simple tubing likely can help you achieve that.

A tiered waterfall is the type of waterfall that incorporates little pools and spills to create an effect of many little waterfalls. This type of waterfall fits well into an informal-style pond within a natural-looking water feature. Think of the side of a large mountain in a state park, with several small waterfalls coursing down the side. For this type of design to work best, the pools situated higher in the configuration should be larger and spill away into the smaller pools. This will create the right amount of volume for the fall and preserve the natural look of the falls.

A single fall is a fall that drops from one point, such as a basin or another drop point, into the body of water. You might also hear it referred to as a curtain fall, or a column fall. Whether you like this type of fall is a matter of personal taste. Some gardeners like the dramatic effect of this rushing drop, while others find it too simple and amateur looking. A single fall can fit in almost any situation. In a contemporary design, a single column of rushing water spilling out of a silver basin can be striking against a stark background. In an informal setting, a rushing fall that emerges from the leaves and blooms is reminiscent of the rain forest.

Streams

If you intend to place a stream with your waterfall or pond, there are options for the stream's placement. The stream can feed into the fall, which can then end in the pond. Or the fall can be midway through the stream, which then continues on. The water that flows down the stream will need a starting and ending point. This can be two ponds or can go in different directions, depending on your design. The stream needs to have enough water flow to support the waterfall. Design it to be proportional to your pond and waterfall. Also, the water will mix as it flows through this setup.

Streams have a layer of gravel or small pebbles over the flexible liner, which gives the stream a nice effect as it flows along. A more formal-looking stream might be walled in by concrete or bricks. The stream needs to be the right depth and slope. The width and depth of your stream are decided by how you want it to look and the flow and speed of water you hope to achieve. A traditional stream only gets a little deeper, and gradually. The depth needs to be right so water will continuously flow along, even though it is not steep. A depth of 5 to 7 inches is ideal. As the stream progresses, it can get deeper, at the rate of about an inch every 10 feet. At the same time, the stream has to be capable of handling the water flow. If you hope to let your fish swim through the stream, you will have to build it wide and deep enough for their comfort. This varies depending on the type of fish. You can consult with the store where you purchase the fish, or research online to find the necessary depth.

Photo courtesy of Drs. Foster and Smith Aquatics

Adding large rocks in the stream's pathway gives a natural feel but can also change the stream's flow. It changes the look and sound of the stream for visitors as the water splashes against the rocks. If you find the stream too quiet, this is an easy way to change it. As with anything else you place in the pond, the rocks will become part of the ecosystem. Algae and other forms of pond life might begin to grow on their undersides.

Creating Your Waterfall

Waterfall creation requires more work and is more difficult than creating a simple pond. You might need to plan more time for the installation of the waterfall. Installing the entire waterfall on your own will be difficult and time consuming. You will likely need helpers to get it installed in a timely fashion.

Choosing a pump

HY-Drive Waterfall pump with a removable clog-resistant housing. Photo courtesy of Drs. Foster and Smith Aquatics

A pump is needed to displace the water over the waterfall. This pump will connect to tubing that will route the water from the body of water back up to the top of the waterfall. Choosing a pump is important because this pump will create the effect over the slope you construct. Submersible pumps are pumps that sit inside the pond. They make less noise and are cheaper than an external pump. External pumps are only suitable for large ponds. Choosing a larger volume pump than is necessary is a good idea. If the pump is too fast or loud, it can be turned down, but a smaller pump might not be able to be turned up to the speed or level you desire. The height of your waterfall will also add to the factors in choosing a pump. A higher waterfall needs a larger volume pump to displace the water that high. *Chapter 2 offers more information on choosing a pump.*

Creating a plan

Creating a plan for a waterfall also can be more difficult than sketching a design for a pond. A formal waterfall will be easier on paper because a natural-styled waterfall is created through experimenting and moving around rocks and boulders.

Perhaps the easiest way to begin planning is to get your basic shapes down. To have a waterfall, you must have a place for the water to fall from and a place for the water to fall into. You have to decide: Will you have two pools, with the water falling from one to the other, a stack of boulders, with tubing directing water down the front into a pond, or a reservoir waterfall, with a hidden stash of water that keeps the feature streamlined and clean?

Once your pond (or two ponds) are dug, you can use edging to help direct the water. Edging plays an important role in the look of a waterfall, perhaps even more so than in the design of a pond. If you are hoping to create a natural-looking waterfall, the placement of rocks and plants around the edges of your falls is critical to achieving that look. In nature, you see rocks surrounding a waterfall, with streams of water running through them to create small, streaming waterfalls. Though these rocks seem to be stacked haphazardly, you already know that Mother Nature is not such a sloppy architect. Stacking the rocks,

Photo courtesy of Drs. Foster and Smith Aquatics

especially the larger boulders, around your pond and fall, with no plan beforehand, can lead to a disaster. But this is an area where you might not want to stick to your plan. After all, a plan is just that. There is no way to know what will look best until you get outside and build. If you are not in a rush to get the fall finished, or if you have a large crowd of helpers, start by placing the largest rocks on the bottom for stability and to hold the liner in place. Then experiment with the smaller rocks in different configurations to accent around the actual fall. The edging also will have to camouflage the tubing that runs from the pond to the top of the waterfall. Depending on the installation method you choose, you could run this tubing underground, or more likely along the bank of your pond, camouflaged from sight with boulders or plants.

Perhaps you have envisioned a tropical-style waterfall, reminiscent of the rain forest, with lush greenery around the water. Just the way that a pond can have plant shelves, your waterfall also can have plant shelves of a sort, flat areas around the pools of water suitable to place a planter on. These plants can be planted in planters, which are complementary colors that camouflage into the waterfall and covered in moss so they blend into the background. Or you can plant marginals that will grow high at the bottom, and in a few seasons they will stretch up to cover what is beyond them, leaving the look of layers of vegetation in the jungle.

The key to creating an authentic-looking waterfall is to have a real-looking flow of water over the entire fall area, with water flowing at a consistent rate so there is no sputtering at any point.

Hiding the tubing, or waterfall box, from which the water is emerging, also is important. The flow must also be consistent with the rest of the pond's look and serve the needs of the pond. A waterfall helps to add oxygen to the pond water, and if its flow is not strong enough, it will not produce enough.

Modifications to the basic waterfall plan

Most waterfalls will follow the same basic plan to be constructed. There is a higher point from which the water falls, a body of water beneath that catches the falling water, a pump that circulates the water, and tubing attached to the pump, which directs the water back to the top of the waterfall. Get creative by re-imagining these elements. Some ideas to get you started:

- Create a pondless waterfall. Traditionally, this is done by replacing the pond area into which the water would normally fall with a small area filled with gravel or rocks. The water flows through these rocks and is then pumped back to the top. If you like this concept but would like

Mini-pondless waterfall kit.
Photo courtesy of Drs. Foster and Smith Aquatics

to be different than the rest of the pack, you can create the rock and gravel area in a different shape or even replace it with a large container. You can dig this area as a small, round area that can then be camouflaged by grasses, or covered with a grate and decorative rocks or shells.

- A vanishing waterfall is the name given to a waterfall that includes a small pond for the water to fall into, which disappears once the pump is turned off. To create this type of design will require a reservoir between the pond and the pump. This is where the water will go when the pump is turned off.

- Take a cue from the statuary fountain and create a statuary fall. The area from which the water fills can be a basin that overflows, or a decorative rock with tubing placed inside so the water emerges from it and falls into the lower lying area.

Observation Point

Large natural waterfalls have an observation point or viewing spot, set far away from the area of danger. This might be a good idea in your yard. Although your friends and family might not set out to cause trouble, and though your pond might not be deep, keeping people away from the direct spill of the waterfall is still a good idea. As a host or hostess, this can also help to keep the chaos and mess of a party to one specific area. It can also help you create a party atmosphere by forcing your guests to talk to one another instead of being in different sections of the yard. When you consider where to place the spot, it will need to be large enough for several people to stand around. People might want to take pictures, so make sure it is a place with good lighting, where the pond's prominent features are displayed. There are different kinds of observation points you can create:

- A bridge or dock on the opposite side of the pond

- A wooden railing around the pond area

- A seating area that allows good viewing of the pond

Photos courtesy of Douglas Brown

Waterfall lights

Solar-powered light used to light up a waterfall at night. Photo courtesy of Douglas Brown

Any visitor to Niagara Falls can tell you the night view of the falls is made completely different by the use of lights. After dark, light is projected into the falls, and it turns it different colors. The effect of the water churning and flowing in the different colors against the night sky is almost magical. Granted, your waterfall will be much smaller, but using lighting to increase the visual effect is still a good idea. Because your waterfall is much smaller, placing light inside the pond to shoot up and out of the water might be the best approach. You might already have plans for lighting around the pond's perimeter or the area of the water feature. Consider the type of lighting you would like to go in the feature and how this lighting will tie in with your design plan. Underwater lights exist specifically for this purpose. You can choose plain lights for a simpler design or colored lights to add extra flair. Submersible lights can be put on a timer or automatically change colors. *Lighting will be discussed in more detail in Chapter 8.*

Double your fun

Creating a feature that holds a fountain and a waterfall might seem like a spectacular idea. But beware of straining your pond with too much. Even a larger pond can be overwhelmed by the noise and movement of the two, especially if two separate pumps are operating them. From a design perspective, you run the risk of cluttering the water feature. Having too complicated of a design can lessen the visual impact of the features. However, if you want both, there are some possible solutions. A fountain with a runoff lip that spills into a larger pond gives the waterfall effect. Or if you have a large yard, you could create two ponds that link together with a stream. A large property might be able to accommodate two separate features, or you could consider breaking them up, perhaps a statuary in the front yard and a waterfall in the back.

Finding Inspiration

Take inspiration from a famous garden, designed by one of the finest artists ever. Half a million tourists visit artist Claude Monet's water garden in Giverny, France, about 45 minutes away from Paris, annually. One-half of the garden is a more traditional garden, with bright blooming flowers. An enthusiastic gardener, but an artist in all he did, Monet chose plants that would fill his garden with pleasing colors. Tulips in vivid violets and blushing pinks are featured in his informal design. Fruit trees grow tall with daisies and grasses tickling at their roots. Iron arches tilt toward the sky, as roses sunbathe along their length. On what used to be the neighbor's adjoining property, Monet created a traditional Japanese design, featuring koi and a small footbridge. Willow trees and wisteria plants give the water garden a soft setting, where light and shade can dance on the water's surface. A Japanese-style bridge, which visitors can still walk across, spans the water.

Design Plan No. 5: A Basic Stream

A stream can be small and winding, connect two bodies to create a more natural look, or be straight and well defined for a more contemporary look.

1. Begin by marking the stream's path. You can use stakes and a rope to mark the watercourse area, or mark the ground with chalk or spray paint. If you are planning a natural-looking stream, you might want to create small shallow pools along the watercourse. Mark these at the same time.

2. Excavate the stream with a shovel or spade. Try to keep the depth of the stream in each section as uniform as possible.

3. Line the excavated waterway with underlayment material and liner. You can use flexible liner cut to size, or strips of flexible liner joined by waterproof tape or glue.

4. Secure the edges of the liner with rocks. These do not have to be permanently placed at this stage. They will keep the liner in place so you can test the watercourse. You can rearrange them to their permanent position once the stream is completed. You can also add rocks into the stream's pathway at that stage.

5. If you have chosen to use a pump to direct the water back up to the top of the stream, you can install the pump and tubing.

Photo courtesy of Douglas Brown

Design Plan No. 6: Stream With Waterfalls

1. Mark the stream's path using stakes and a rope. Stake wider sections along the course to create small shallow pools, from which the waterfalls will happen. Check to make sure the stream's width is consistent, unless you intend to vary the width to slow down and speed up the water's flow along the stream.

2. Excavate the stream's marked path with a shovel or spade. As you reach each fall section, excavate the next piece of stream at a slightly deeper depth.

3. Line the excavated waterway with liner. Given the shallower depth of a stream, underlayment material is not necessary. You can use a thin section of liner or strips of liner glued or taped together.

4. Place gravel or pebbles along the course of the stream, on top of the flexible liner. This will give the stream a pebbled flow, similar to the natural stream.

5. Install the pump. Connect the pump to the plastic tubing that will direct water back to the head of the stream. Place the body of the pump in the base pool, and run the tubing along the side of the stream. Cover this exposed tubing with dirt, moss, rocks, plants, or whatever edging you will be using.

6. Fill the pond or reservoir feeding the stream with water. If you are going to test the pump at this time, turn it on and let it run for a while. As it runs, try the different flows and settings. Experiment with the edging materials to make sure the tubing is hidden.

CHAPTER 6

An Introduction to Water Gardening

Depending on the gardener's preference, the garden can take on different looks. The look can also change each season or change completely each year with the addition of new plants. As the gardener evolves, so does the garden, and as the years go by, the plants will come back lusher and fuller.

Perhaps more than any other one part, the garden sets the expectation of styling and look for the visitor. Large lush green plants might remind viewers of the rainforest, while perfectly manicured roses and cannas give the look of a more formal and stylized garden. Use the plants to complement the other components of the garden. If you are creating a bog garden and want a natural look, reminiscent of nearby wilderness, stock local, native plants. In a garden where the water feature is meant to be the star of the show, smaller, simpler plants can frame the feature without detracting from the focus.

In most cases, plants will be included in your pond design from the beginning. After all, it is difficult to imitate the look of a lush garden or a natural lake without plants to make it look authentic.

What is Water Gardening?

As with gardening in your yard or in planters filled with potting soil, water gardening is about achieving a happy balance of conditions that allow and encourage your plants to grow. However, when water gardening, there are more factors to consider.

Plants are more than just flowers or blooms and, in a pond, serve more than an aesthetic purpose. A basic thing that separates a pond from other bodies of water is its acceptance of fauna. Before filters and chemical supplements existed, plants within an ecosystem kept the water in balance, cleaning out the toxins and maintaining the natural pH. This is why it is important to choose the right plants in the right quantities. They will each have an effect on the balance of the pond, and if too many of one kind are present, they will put the pond out of balance. In addition to balancing the pond, plants also provide cover and shade that will cool your pond and fish on hot days. The surface cover they create also will help to control the algae population in your pond because algae prefer sunlight to grow in. Too much algae in the pond can lead to a green pond or a slimy pond. You will also need to monitor the plant growth carefully to make sure certain plants do not take over. It also will take extra time and work to restore the balance of the pond if an invasive plant is introduced and takes over. In the case of a stubborn pest, such as duckweed, you might not be able to eradicate it and will end up with a green pond.

Algae

Another factor to consider when debating adding plants to your pond is algae. Some of these algae will be helpful to the health of the pond. Without enough plants in the water, you run the risk of having a green pond. Unchecked, algae will grow at an amazing rate. Controlling the algae growth through the use of other plants will take time, which is why you might not want to wait until you have an algae problem before considering other plants. A mix of plants from each category will help you to combat algae growth.

If algae growth gets out of hand, algicide can be purchased from the pond supply store. This is a chemical that will kill algae. However, if your pond is still out of balance, you might end up with the same problem again.

There are some factors to consider when debating adding plants to your current pond design:

- **Time:** Introducing plants to your pond will require work on your part. In addition to researching and shopping for the plants and planting supplies, you will have to re-pot the plants into appropriate water-ready containers. For the first few weeks, you will have to monitor the plants carefully to see which ones are surviving and which are failing. Along with the time it takes to add the plants, being a water gardener automatically adds to the amount of weekly care and maintenance your water feature requires. The good news is there are plants you can choose that will require less time from you on a regular basis. But you will also need to add time for seasonal maintenance, for example, removing tropical plants from the pond each winter and bringing them inside. There will also be care, such as thinning and re-potting.

- **Cost:** Stocking a pond with plants comes with a cost. In addition to the cost of the plants, you will need planting baskets, burlap or foam to line the basket, and soil and gravel to fill the basket, and you might need pond supplements to cure any imbalances in the pond's ecosystem at first. Some plants will require fertilizer tablets to grow strong and adapt to the pond environment. Depending on the plants you choose, the cost involved can vary. The more expensive plants also tend to be the more fragile tropical plants, but these will add the most color and allure to your garden. If you prefer to stay local, check with your nursery for native plants that will offer good color.

- **Larger problems:** You are creating more than a water feature; you are creating a whole ecosystem. Introducing plants into a pond can create problems until the ecosystem finds it own balance. The chemicals or nitrates these plants emit might cause an imbalance in the pond, which might require treatment. Some plants are more invasive and might overtake the pond's surface. Aggressive plants could be difficult or impossible to eradicate from your pond.

- **Fish and animals:** The addition of more plants to your pond will draw more animals to the pond area. Flowering plants will attract insects and small birds. If you have created an area where you can sit by and enjoy, extra bugs might hamper your fun, particularly in the summertime. In some places, you can expect frogs and reptiles attracted by the water and moist grass. Depending on where you live, you might have to worry about raccoons and predatory birds, such as herons, that will hang around your pond and stalk your fish.

If you hope to achieve a natural look, adding plants is necessary. A pond with no plants around the edges gives itself away as the work of an amateur landscaper. After all, a pond is just a hole in the ground, filled with water.

What elevates it to a beautiful design element are the edges and extras you add to it and the atmosphere you create with these tools. Plants are the easiest and most cost-effective way to give any design a natural feel.

In nature, the change from the shore to water is gradual. Think of the way the sand at the beach slopes gradually under the water's edge, or the way a pond's water is buffeted by reeds and tall grasses. In some places, a mountain or outcropping of boulders rises to meet the water's edge. Do not make the line where the plants stop and the water begins a stark contrast unless you are hoping to create a formal design. As you plan the pond, consider the heights each plant will grow to and how that will affect the look of the pond over time.

Water-Friendly Plants

Having made the decision to add plants, take some time to familiarize yourself with the different kinds of pond plants available. Research the plants native to your local area and figure out which of the following categories they fall into. It is advisable to use local plants. They are ready for your climate and weather conditions and will stay in proportion with other local plants in your ecosystem. You might have experience with plants in your garden, and though that is a plus, you will see some differences between regular gardening in soil and water gardening, which can include plants that root in soil, and plants that prefer to spread their roots across the water. Different materials are required for different types of plants. Unless you are creating a bog or marsh, most of your plants will need to go in planting baskets or underwater potting plants.

Floating plants

Water hyacinth.

Floating plants, as the name implies, like to go where the pond water takes them. They do best when they are allowed to let their roots float in the water without a basket hampering them. As their leaves dance across the pond's surface, the roots are helping the pond's ecosystem. Smaller organisms, such as larvae, can live on the roots, and larger pond animals can get shade in the roots of the plant. Some pond animals and organisms will even feed off these roots. If you choose to stock your pond with fish, the floating plants will provide them with a home. Although it is not ideal, you can choose to plant a floating plant in a container to keep it from growing too big. If it is an invasive plant, this might help to contain the plant's growth. Floating plants will spread quickly but are easily removed from the pond, unless they are invasive. Water hyacinth, a lovely looking floater that flowers, is also an invasive plant that causes major problems in the ecosystems of the southern states' waterways.

Examples of floating plants are water lettuce and water poppy.

What about water lilies?

Many gardeners think of the water lily as a floating plant because they have seen its large leaves floating on the water's surface. However, unlike floating plants with trailing roots, the water lily has thick, tuber roots. Because of this, the water lily is not suited to floating around in the water and needs its roots contained in a pot or basket. This is why the

Photo courtesy of Douglas Brown

water lily is referred to as a floating leaf plant and not a floating plant. There are two basic types of water lilies: the tropical water lily or the hardy water lily. Tropical lilies, as the name suggests, prefer a warm climate for blooming. Hardy lilies, as their name suggests, can tolerate a slightly colder climate. Under these two umbrellas, there are hundreds of different lilies varying in color and smell. *For more specifics on lily varieties, see Appendix B.* Because lilies like to have their roots submerged and the leaves floating on the surface, you might have to place their basket on a shelf until they grow longer.

Marginal Plants

Iris flowers.

If you hope to create a smooth, seamless transition from land to water, marginal plants are your new best friend. Marginals like to live along the water's edge where they can reach into the water. These are the kinds of plants you can place on the shelves around the edges of your pond. With time and care, some will grow to stand tall, their stalks emerging from the water and hiding the pond's edge from sight. Others will grow close to the ground and spread wider, hiding the pond's liner from sight. These will help give your pond the look of a well-established, natural occurrence. Plants you would see along the banks of a river or pond, such as reeds and grass, fall into this category. Some flowering plants, such as irises and marigold, also fall into this category. Most marginal plants want 6 to 9 inches of water to live in, at the most. Alternatively, you can place these plants on a stack of bricks within the pond if you want to have them in different locations, but they still might not like that prolonged exposure to water.

Submerged Plants

Submerged plants are also known as oxygenators because they create and supply oxygen for the plants and animals in the pond. These plants process carbon dioxide and disperse oxygen, which is the opposite of what humans do when they breathe. Too many of these plants might be too much of a good thing, as too much oxygen will also damage the ecosystem and lead to plant problems. You will find they require cutting back more regularly than other plants. Similar to algae, submerged plants spread quickly

Hornwort is an example of a submerged plant.

and provide food and important nutrients for pond fish. Submerged plants will do best under the water's surface. A basket will contain the roots if you do not want them to spread or take root on the bottom of the pond. Because different kinds of oxygenators will produce oxygen at different intervals, it might be best to choose a variety of submerged plants so the water is constantly kept stocked with oxygen. Submerged plants also will help you control algae growth. They process the nitrogen in pond water, due to the fish waste and decayed leaves in the water. This is the same nitrogen algae need to grow.

Bog plants

Cattails planted in a bog along a pond's edge.

Bog or marsh plants are more like traditional garden plants because they like to be planted directly in soil. But for these plants, not just any soil will do. These plants prefer a moist, soggy soil, and do not do well in a dry environment. That is why a bog, where the soil is not allowed to get too dry, is the ideal place for them. They can be planted in a marginal bog, along the edge of a pond, or in a separate bog garden. Unlike most of the other pond plants, bog plants should not be planted in a container but directly in the soil. *Bogs are discussed in more detail in Chapter 3.*

Some examples of bog plants are Cattail and canna.

Non-native and invasive plants

From the unpleasant name, you might envision invasive plants to be ugly. But many invasive plants are beautiful. Some produce beautiful, brightly colored flowers you might be used to seeing in nature. Invasive plants are not native to the area they wreak havoc in, so they cannot be blamed.

They do not have any natural predators to cull their growth. Nothing hampers their progress as they drain and clog the waterways, forcing local birds and other animals to find another habitat. In many places, local government officials are taking steps to ban invasive species of plants in the area. This can result in a fine if a banned plant from your garden is introduced into the wild. Check with your local officials, such as the county or parks and recreation department, to find out which plants are termed invasive or banned. Their growth cannot be contained, so it is important to check before introducing a plant into your pond to make sure that it is not invasive. Once introduced to your pond, an invasive plant will take over and eat the nutrients in your pond water so it cannot sustain other plants. Some pond plants are persistent and require you to empty and flush the whole pond out.

Opinions differ on whether there is a need to introduce an invasive plant to your pond because some of them do serve a purpose. Duckweed, for example, makes fish food. It is also one of the hardest plants to chase out of a pond once introduced. Every speck of the plant will need to be flushed from the pond for this to work, so you might have to flush it multiple times.

For some invasive plants, once they are removed, you must also be careful about how you dispose of them. If any of the plant makes its way into the wild, it could be devastating to the local ecosystem. Even if you do not intend to let it go into the wild, some of these plants can be transmitted in other ways, such as when a bird visits a plant in your pond and then visits a flower in a local lake. In the extreme case, it can drive other plants away and destroy the natural habitat of local animals. Many invasive plants can be classified in other categories. For example, duckweed and water hyacinth are floating plants and invasive.

Be careful, and take the time to research your plants before introducing them to your pond because pond and garden stores still sell invasive plants. Also, beware of uneducated gardeners. An easy way to introduce an invasive plant without intending to is by taking plants from a well-meaning friend or neighbor. Worse still is snipping flowers or plants from a lake without knowing their type or name.

Water lettuce. Photo courtesy of United States Geological Survey Nonindigenous Aquatic Species

Examples of invasive plants are water lettuce and kudzu.

Choosing Your Plants

Before you bring a plant into your pond environment, do some quick investigating. Inspect the roots of any plant you plan to put in your pond, regardless of whether it is coming from a store, a friend, or the wild. Check that the roots look strong, well hydrated, and not brittle. Look for insects or any type of rot or disease on the plant's root system or stalks.

Ask before you buy

Do not be afraid to ask questions before you purchase plants for your pond. After all, this is not different than any other purchase. It is just like a trip to the electronics or furniture store. Asking questions will help you determine if you are talking to another gardener or a salesperson with basic knowledge of the product. Beware of nurseries that are not receptive to your questions. The best nurseries are happy to have knowledgeable gardeners purchasing their products and bringing them to fruition. They should be able to tell you the type and name of each plant and its recommended care and temperature.

Tropical versus hardy plants

Whether you choose tropical or hardy plants is dependent on your local climate and your available time and experience as a gardener. At this point, you might also want to consult the USDA's Plant Hardiness Zone Map to identify the zone you live in and the plants that can live in that climate. This map is a useful tool that many gardeners use to help them select plants. Using this tool is an easy way to eliminate failing plants and choosing the wrong plants, which will waste your time and money, and for a new gardener, this can lead to frustration. Tropical plants are plants best suited to a warm climate because they want a certain amount of sunlight each day and a certain water temperature. Some are so sensitive they will wilt away after only a few days of a colder temperature, so if your weather is known to be unpredictable, consider carefully before purchasing these.

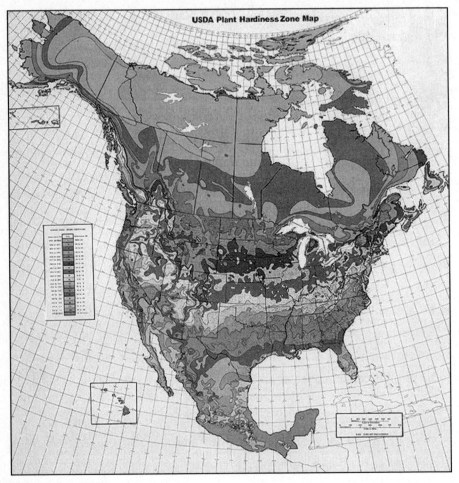

Map courtesy of USDA

Introducing Plants to Your Pond

Because your pond is going to be a whole ecosystem, introducing plants to the pond is more than just placing them inside the feature. The timing of when you place the plants into the feature is important. If the feature is new, give the water a few weeks to settle. The water will need to be decalcified and start generating bacteria. The bacteria have to make their way to the filter and circulate in the pond to make it ready for plants and

Photo courtesy of Drs. Foster and Smith

Picturesque Ponds

Photo courtesy of Drs. Foster and Smith

Photo courtesy of Drs. Foster and Smith

Photo courtesy of Drs. Foster and Smith

Photo courtesy of Drs. Foster and Smith

Photo courtesy of Drs. Foster and Smith

Photo courtesy of Drs. Foster and Smith

Photo courtesy of Drs. Foster and Smith

Photo courtesy of Drs. Foster and Smith

IX

X

Photo courtesy of Drs. Foster and Smith

XIII

Photo courtesy of Drs. Foster and Smith

A special thank you to Drs. Foster and Smith for providing
many photographs for this book.

fish. This is a good time to make sure the pond does not have any leaks and to test the water's pH to make sure it is neutral and remains stable.

The outdoor temperature and time of year are also important. Pay attention to the temperature requirement for each plant and the time of year it is expected to bloom. This information will come on labels, packaging, or tags that come with the plants you purchase. You might be inclined to throw away these items because they will not stay organized and will likely become clutter. Before doing so, think about preserving the information, whether in a binder, spreadsheet, or on index cards. Record the name and type of the plant, the date and location of the store you purchased it from, the date you introduced it to the pond, and the recommended care of the plant. You can also include extra information that you might have relevant to this plant, such as tips you found online or got from friends about this plant. This will save you return trips to the garden store or nursery.

After introducing the plants, you will have to monitor them carefully to see which ones are taking well to the new environment and which need help. Some of your plants will fail, which is why it is advisable to start with cheaper plants and add more expensive blooms later, when you are more experienced as a water gardener and have a better idea about how they will react.

Fertilizing Your Pond Plants

Some, or all if you feel it necessary, of your plants can benefit from fertilizer. If you live in a zone where the season for plants to bloom is short, you might want to do something to encourage your blooms to come out sooner or stronger. Fertilizer is available in different forms:

- Fertilizer tablets, which are put directly into the soil in the plant's basket. You can insert these in the middle of the pot when re-potting your plants, and some will last all season. For those who find they need to fertilize regularly, take the plant out of the pond and press the tablet down into the soil of the basket. Some gardeners find fertilizer spikes, meant for use on tomato plants, to be more economical and easier to find.

- Liquid plant fertilizer poured directly into the pond. The fertilizer is then absorbed by the plants through the roots. There are also dissolvable fertilizers you can put in the water.

- Plants that can be removed from the pond, such as floating plants, can be removed and the roots soaked in liquid plant fertilizer for as long as three days. Rinse the roots thoroughly, and put them back in the pond. Because this type of fertilizer is not safe to put directly in pond water, make sure you remove as much of this from the roots as you can. Do not pour this type of fertilizer directly in the pond.

- Gardeners who have a better understanding of plant chemistry can construct their own plant spikes, containing phosphorous, potassium, and other elements. If you are someone who hopes to experiment with your own formulas for fertilizer, this is a good way to begin.

Fertilizer can be added anytime you wish to grow more, or larger, blooms on your flowers. Most pond fertilizers are safe for pond fish. But too much can promote algae growth. They can leave you with an algae problem, which can be hard to get rid of. To avoid this, try to resist the temptation to fertilize too much.

Capturing the Moments

Creating, installing, and keeping a pond is a big achievement with work involved, and it is something of which you can be proud. Why not document it in a way that other people can follow your progress and accomplishments? There are easy ways to do this:

Journal: Keep a photo journal documenting the growth of your project each week or month. Take before and after pictures of the site where your pond is going to be. As your plants grow, take pictures each week or each month to show how much they grow. If you hope to stay green, use your computer to organize your thoughts and photos.

Blog: If you hope to share your knowledge or experience, consider creating an online blog where fellow gardeners can visit and offer advice. As your readership grows, you will learn more tips and tricks from every corner. Doing this also will provide you with a handy, free backup of all the pictures and information you have stored about your pond on your computer, just in case anything ever happens to those files.

Join: If you do not have enough time to maintain your own website, online gardening communities abound where you can post your pictures, ask and answer questions, and connect with gardening enthusiasts all over. This is much less work than a blog; it requires you only to stop in when the opportunity arises. Or consider joining a community gardening group to exchange tips and information.

Building Your Ecosystem

Now that you have created the pond and decided to include plants and perhaps even animals, you will be building a complicated and sensitive thing: an ecosystem. All the elements in your pond will have to exist in harmony and balance. To maintain the ecosystem's balance, you will have to monitor and observe the pond carefully and regularly.

This will require time and attention to detail, which is why the installation of the pond stretches beyond the day you dig and fill the pond. Think of a choir singing a beautiful classic. For the song to sound perfect, each part must be sung in perfect harmony. In a pond, each component must be in balance for the whole pond to be healthy and beautiful. If only half the sopranos in a choir are hitting the high notes, the song will sound good but not as beautiful as it could. Try as they might to compensate, the altos and tenors will not sound as good. Similar, if only half your submerged plants are producing the maximum amount of oxygen, the pond will not be as clear and balanced as it could be. Although they will try to do their jobs within the pond as best they can, the other plants will not be as healthy and flourishing as they could be.

Within the ecosystem, the fish will be responsible for eating the algae and possibly other pests, such as mosquito larvae. The fish will produce waste, which contains ammonia, and bacteria will convert this waste into other chemicals. The plants, meanwhile, are charged with creating oxygen for the fish, and they also process fish waste. All these jobs have to happen at the right time, and in the right proportion, for the pond to stay in balance.

Aquatic plants can be placed in baskets or pots with drainage holes. For plants that are going to end up in the pond, there are some additional options. Aquatic plants pots are similar to regular planting pots, but they do not have drainage holes. They are championed by those who find baskets a mess and hate getting any soil in the pond area. An aquatic plant pot, with no drainage holes, along with a layer of clay or gravel on top, does not allow

AquaPlanter. Photo courtesy of Drs. Foster and Smith Aquatics

any soil to seep out. There also are fabric baskets, which are similar to using a basket but without the plastic exterior. They are simply soft baskets, made of burlap or a similar material. Many gardeners find these combine the best of both worlds, but others find they are unstable and difficult to manipulate if you wish to change their location around the pond.

Soil matters

What kind of soil will fare best in your pond? Should you use regular old soil from your yard or brand new expensive stuff from the store? Regular potting soil from the home improvement store or soil from your garden is not the right choice. Neither of these has the weight needed to keep the plant, and the nutrients the plants need, inside the pot. Also, soil from your garden might contain pesticides that can prove toxic to your pond plants or fish. If you choose to use potting soil, make sure it is a heavy kind. There is special aquatic soil available, which holds together better in the basket than potting soil will. You can even use clay soil, which will hold together well inside the basket, but it can be too heavy.

Lotus magic

If your pond flowers are stars, think of the lotus as your prima donna leading lady. Beautiful? Yes. Demanding? Perhaps. Sensitive? Yes. The lotus, like a Hollywood starlet, demands perfect lighting, more than three months' worth of 80-degree weather, to be exact. Like a well-paid supermodel, the lotus will not open her petals on just any day. Most lotuses have a three-day blooming cycle, during which the large petals will open and expand, to a maximum span of several feet. Like any true star, the lotus packs a wow factor, a beautiful color that can only be truly enjoyed during the three days it blooms.

Water Garden Intruders

Just as pests and animals will try to undo your hard work in a regular garden, there are pests and animals that will target your aquatic plants. Turtles will slice happily into aquatic plants and leave you wondering who cut your plant leaves with scissors. Do not blame neighborhood children or vandals for this. Getting the turtle out of your pond is the best solution to this problem, but be careful of your fingers because a turtle will nip at your fingers with its sharp teeth and stinging bite. If you introduce koi into your pond, they might munch on your plants, even though you feed them. They particularly like to eat pond lilies, which can be frustrating given the extra cost and effort involved with these flowers. Snails might find their way into the pond and cut what look like small holes in the leaves. Though they might eat the plants, they also will eat dirt and debris out of the pond and a more annoying pest, insects.

Insects also are likely to become a pest to your pond. Aphids are small black insects that look round, like lice. They are called plant lice. They can also be white or even pink. Aphids might start to show up on the leaves that sprout from your plants or on the near dead ones. They might burrow down into the plant's roots. Many gardeners use simple water to remove aphids, a technique that might work, depending on how many aphids have made their way into the pond. Simply rinsing off the stalks of the affected plant might take care of a small infestation. Gardeners with a larger infestation will need to overflow the pond, or run water into the pond so the water runs over the edge, similar to the recommended treatment for duckweed. Depending on the ecological concerns of the gardener, a simpler solution might exist. If the aphids are only on a few plants, removing these plants and treating them with insecticide might do the trick and create less of a mess. Rinse the plants well before returning them to the pond.

Birds might also come to visit your pond. If you hope to encourage them, you can plant the kinds of plants you know will attract them. Plants with berries, such as mulberries and blackberries, or flowers, such as sunflowers and marigolds, will entice birds to the area. It also helps if they have easy access through a clear entrance point or perhaps a birdbath close by, so the bird can observe the whole setup before coming down to the pond.

CASE STUDY: DESIGNING A NATURAL HABITAT

Cassy Aoyagi
President
FormLA Landscaping
www.formla.com
Note: Cassy is also the president of
the Theodore Payne Foundation for
Wildflowers and Native Plants.

There is obvious charm to the sound and aesthetic water features provide, but my primary goal is attracting life and nature. Water is a critical element to creating a complete "wildlife" habitat. In a wildlife habitat, plants provide food and shelter, and water provides the life source and the basis for the food chain. This food chain allows wildlife and habitats to thrive in an outdoor space. All pond water is domestic water. The most challenging aspect is over-chlorination, which takes ponds out of balance and kills fish. De-chlorinators help. Also, when replenishing water, we recommend slow and/or staggered additions of domestic water.

In Southern California, summer evaporation presents the biggest challenge. In some climates, water evaporates so quickly that the amount of chlorinated domestic water needed to replenish a pond can have an adverse effect on the fish. For established ponds, we keep auto-fills to the lowest setting during hot summers and in the hotter micro-climates. If we design a system, we look to provide the pond a balance of sun and shade to avoid overexposure to sun in the summer and too much shade in the winter.

Although it takes upfront time to get things into balance, once balance is achieved, basic maintenance and minimal additives are necessary. Less is truly more. Be careful to consider the effect of all landscaping activities on the pond's health; chemical fertilizers or pesticides that run off into a delicate system can kill plants, animals, and fish or create undesirable algae blooms.

Different bird, bug, reptile, plant, and fish species will want to partake in this living and breathing system. Proactively creating places for the most desirable of them to live, thrive, and protect themselves from natural predators requires thoughtful design that mimics the challenges and support nature provides. Wildlife need hiding places to thrive.

My clients seek the visual pleasure, pleasant sounds, nature drawn to water habitats, and the knowledge they are supporting environmental health. Some have chosen not to pursue water features due to the features' intense appeal to unwanted wildlife.

FormLA Landscaping designs, builds, and maintains custom water features, including waterfalls, stream beds, and biological ponds throughout Los Angeles County. In addition to delivering a sense of serenity to garden spaces, waterfalls, stream beds, and ponds can provide practical benefits. We use water features to facilitate infiltration, which protects homes with slide-prone slopes or to prevent runoff for the good of the city and our ocean health. As professionals, we place our clients on at least an every-other-week maintenance schedule to ensure their biological system thrives. Site drainage, grading, design, and capacity measurement are important critical factors to ensuring a water feature thrives and, ideally, protects and does not endanger homes or other structures. Accredited landscaping professionals should be well versed in making these calculations.

Size recommendations vary based on intended use and the size of the project. Most consider less than 25 square feet to be water sensitive or efficient. If goals for the pond include the catchment, percolation, or storage of water, size will be critical and will require intense and accurate calculations to determine how many gallons it will hold with grace. Look, sound, and wildlife interests are considerations. The same amount of maintenance is needed at any size, so this need not be a deciding factor.

Disease

Plants, like any other living thing, can get sick. Fungal diseases spread quickly in plants and can take down a previously healthy plant to the root. Root rot is an example of a fungal disease that can be devastating to the plant and any other plants that catch the fungus. The disease is introduced through a fungus, from another plant. But fungal diseases also thrive in certain conditions, and you can discourage growth of fungus by taking the following steps to make your pond inhospitable for them:

- Monitor the level of oxygen in the pond, and make sure there is not too much. Too much oxygen will help fungus find a home in your pond.

- Check the recommended level of water for each plant, and make sure each one is in the right amount of water. Too much or too little water can be damaging to your plants.

- Consider the length of time the plant has been in the water. Was the plant introduced to the pond too fast? This can make the plant more susceptible to fungal disease.

- Reflect on the source of the plant. Did you get this plant from a new supplier, a friend, or from the wild?

Removing the plant from the water might solve the problem. Take the plant out of the water, and monitor the new growth and roots to see if they look healthier. Did you introduce any new plants to the feature recently, and if so, did you inspect the roots of this plant before putting it in your pond? If not, the disease might have been introduced with the plant. Remove this plant, and treat it.

Chemicals in the water

The only solution to some plant diseases, parasite or insect infestations, or imbalance in the pond water might be chemical treatments. As someone who toils in the garden, you might be concerned about how introducing chemicals will affect your pond and the environment. Why create a beautiful, natural pond only to put chemicals in it? First, rest assured that a little chemical goes a long way, so the amount that will end up in your pond is small. If you have concerns about using chemicals, avoid them as much as possible. Use them only as a last resort, after first trying insecticides made with natural organisms. Chemical-based pesticides can be harmful to the plants and animals in the pond, while insecticides that use natural bacteria are not. They can be less effective, which is why the pesticides exist. Be sure to follow the instructions. Most pesticides require the plant to be removed from the pond for treatment. Remove the plants to treat them, and rinse them off before returning them to the pond.

Family Activity: Create Your Own Floating Islands

Getting your children excited and involved in water gardening will benefit them in many ways. Seeing the plants grow and helping you balance the pond can help them understand chemistry and science concepts they learn in the classroom. Better yet, they can spend quality time with you, out in the fresh air, away from TV and video games.

If you have been a traditional gardener, your children will already be familiar with the idea of planting in soil. A creative way to introduce them to water gardening is to make floating islands for your plants on which to sail across the water. If you want to encourage creativity, you can supply some of the basic materials and let them put the components together to create their own type of island.

Start by getting small plastic pots for the plants. Alternately, window screen can contain the plants. You can use Styrofoam to keep the plants afloat. You might also need some type of waterproof adhesive or spray expandable foam to join the containers together. Depending on the level of responsibility of your children, you might have them devise their islands, then come to you to help put them together. Check to make sure the "design" is stable and not too easy to tip over.

The concept behind the floating island is simple. The plant container will need to stay afloat. It can be decorated after assembly to match the look of the pond. You can join plastic pots joined with anything that will float. Expanding foam can be sprayed on the pots, and when it dries, it will hold the pots in place. Pool noodles will wrap around the planters and keep them afloat, but they tend to deteriorate easily with exposure to sunlight.

Plants can be set into window screens instead of plant pots. This leaves the roots of the plant available under the water's surface for your fish to nibble and snack on. At the same time, this will contain the plant better than a floating plant left on the surface. Then, the window screen can be made buoyant in the same ways the potting plants can with Styrofoam or spray foam. You can paint the island with nontoxic paint or cover it with fabric. Fabric is not likely to last as long because the sun and water exposure will break it down.

If you have the technical knowledge and tools, you can carve a larger piece of wood to hold a plant in the middle. Once they are involved in the project, your children might surprise you with the items they suggest as potential islands. Just about anything that will contain the plant and stay afloat could work, so feel free to experiment with just about anything, as long as you are sure it will not be harmful to your fish.

CHAPTER 7

Swimming Under
the Surface

Observing fish in a pond is a different situation than observing fish in an aquarium. Watching fish in a pond is a pleasant way to pass the time, but it is also an indication of the health and success of your pond. Over time, you will notice the behavior patterns of your fish. You might see them spawn and create new life. The fish in a pond rely on you in a different way than

Photo courtesy of Drs. Foster and Smith Aquatics

indoor aquarium fish. These fish need you to create a healthy habitat for them to thrive in. When watching them, you get the double satisfaction of a job well done in caring for the fish and in building the ecosystem in which they live.

Pond fish are available in different sizes, colors, and species. Their cost will vary along with their type and pedigree, from simple goldfish that cost a few dollars, up to $10,000 for a prizewinning koi. Although it is better to purchase your fish locally, you might be able to get a better price online.

Research your local options, though. Local fish farms might be able to cut you a better price or might help you if you have a problem with the fish after you get them home, which an online retailer is likely not going to do.

Before heading out to shop for the fish, figure out if your pond is a good home for them. Determining if your pond can support fish is a key first step. If the pond is not a hospitable environment, any fish you stock it with will be a waste of time, money, and life.

Is Your Pond a Good Habitat?

At the outset, it seems like any pond is a good habitat for fish. After all, fish like water; that is from where the expression comes. But following that same line of thought, you do not see fish in ditches or puddles. There are certain things the fish need to survive. A fish pond needs to have the following elements:

- **Plants:** Plants are incredibly useful in multiple ways in the fish pond. They can serve as toilet, habitat, and food source for your fish. First, they will act as a supplement to your filter. They will help to keep the fish healthy by processing their waste. In some cases, plants provide fish with a stable habitat and a food source. Some fish will feast on algae. A plant with large floating leaves provides fish with protection from the sun and from predatory birds or animals.

- **Size:** Fish, depending on their type, will require a certain amount of space to move around and live in. Depending on the size of your pond, you might have to restrict the amount of fish you add. Do not try to overstock your pond because this can lead to problems with the fish. Research how many fish can go in a pond of your capacity, and do not exceed this figure unless you want to lose some fish to overly high ammonia levels or other problems.

- **Age:** A new pond is not ready for fish to live in yet. Tap water contains chlorine, chloramine, and heavy metals. These substances make the water potable for humans but make it less than ideal for pond fish. Let the pond settle for about two weeks to a month. This will allow the water to balance itself to a better habitat for fish. You will have time to treat the water to get the chlorine out and decalcify it, and good bacteria will have time to grow. Your filter will have time to accumulate the bacteria needed to process fish waste, and you will have less risk of ammonia overload when you add the fish.

- **Stability:** Fish need a harmonious environment with stable water conditions. If you are still doing experimenting or making modifications, it might not be the best time to add fish. Fish can be added later.

- **Waterfalls and fountains:** You can add fish to a pond that has a waterfall or fountain in it. But certain fish do not like to be in the area where the water is being displaced. The size of your pond will again factor in here. Is your pond big enough to allow fish an area to rest without being in the area where water is displaced?

Tap Water

Most people will fill the pond with tap water because it is the easiest way to fill a pond, but tap water is not ready for fish to live in. Chlorine is an irritant to fish; it causes irritation to their bodies. The chloramine in water combines chlorine and ammonia, a substance that cannot be in abundance in your water. These two substances, and the metals that can be present in water, must be treated before fish can live a healthy life in this water. Most pond supply stores stock a chemical treatment to turn tap water into pond water. These are inexpensive and easy to use. You can pour this in at the time of filling, and then let the pond sit for at least two weeks. During that time, bacteria will accumulate in the pond. If you have filled your pond with some kind of untreated water, such as well water, you do not have to worry about this.

Fish and mosquitoes

Mosquitoes like stagnant water, and one of the easiest ways to prevent the pond from being overrun with mosquito larvae is to stock the pond with fish. Certain fish will eat the mosquito larvae before they even have a chance to hatch. There are fish called mosquito fish that will eat up the larvae quickly. They might not interact well with other fish in the pond, but they will get along with most. There are also other ways to reduce mosquito presence in your pond. Mosquitoes like standing water, so another easy way to eliminate the potential of being overrun with mosquitoes is to create water movement. If you do not already have a waterfall or fountain, consider adding one because the movement of the water will discourage larvae growth. As your pond matures, amphibians that eat insects will come to it and assist you with bug removal. If you live in an area where mosquitoes abound naturally, consider keeping citronella candles or tiki torches around the pond seating area so your guests will be comfortable.

Choosing Your Fish

Maybe you already have some fish in mind for your pond because you like the look of them, they match the look of the pond, or fit the style you are hoping to present in your garden. It is fine to like fish based on aesthetic reasons, but choose them based on information and knowledge.

Photo courtesy of Drs. Foster and Smith Aquatics

Some of the fish you like will not be able to sustain the temperature in your pond. Others might feast on the plants you have just spent all season growing and nurturing.

Learn as much as you can before you buy fish. Even more than choosing plants, selecting fish is a decision best made informed. Just as with the plants, you need to know the conditions fish prefer, their preferred location within the pond, how they will behave, and with what other kinds they will interact. Also, consider the cost of the fish and the food they prefer to see if it is worth the expense to you. Spend time getting to know the different kinds of fish and the type of environment, care, and food they require. Stocking your pond with fish will be an expensive and time-consuming process, and to lose then due to lack of knowledge would be a shame. You might want to start by purchasing a cheap, hardy fish that will be easy to care for. These fish can serve as an introduction to keeping pond fish, and you can add more expensive, exotic fish later. This also will help to ensure you do not overstock the pond with too many fish at first, a common mistake first-time fish keepers make. Fewer is better, so only purchase a few fish at a time. You might find these fish turn out to be enough for you and there is no need to add more. The fish will spawn under the right conditions, so you might have more in a few seasons.

After deciding what kind of fish you might like, take a trip to the store to see them in person. Observe the fish in their habitat at the store. This is not a natural environment for the fish, and they will not behave as they will in the pond. But healthy fish will still look full-bodied and swim around in the tank. They should respond to you observing them in some way, whether by swimming toward you or just looking back at you as you observe them. Also, take some time to talk with the store's staff to see how knowledgeable about the fish they are. Some fish can be grown locally, while other, more exotic fish will be transported a long way before being sold. It is preferable to buy locally raised fish where you can because traveling stresses the fish. However, not every fish can be grown in every climate, so you will likely end up buying at least a few fish that were grown outside your local area. If the fish have traveled a long way, most reputable sellers will quarantine the fish for a short time before putting them out for sale to be sure they do not have any diseases and are less stressed. Inquire before you buy about whether the store quarantines the fish and for how long they quarantine them. Your experience with fish keeping will dictate how significant this quarantine period is to you. If you have not had a costly outbreak of disease that wipes out your fish, you might not be bothered by the lack of quarantine period. But if you have had a bad experience in your past with a contagious fish disease, you are not going to want to purchase fish that have not had at least a few days of a quarantine period.

Should You Quarantine Your Fish?

After bringing the fish home from the store, you might choose to quarantine them again before introducing them to the pond. Many experienced pond keepers take this extra step, having experienced the negative effects of a new fish with disease. Even if the fish are totally healthy, the stress of changing habitat many times, from the farm where they were raised to the pet store to your pond, can wear on them, which makes them more susceptible to damage once they arrive in their new home. To quarantine the fish at home, set them up alone in a tank filled with de-chlorinated water, or water from the pond if you have tested it recently and are sure it is safe for the fish. This is the best option. The tank will need a filter and might need a heater, depending on the species of fish. Keep the fish quarantined as long as you can, at least for a few days, and watch to make sure they do not show any disease or problems. Depending on the species of fish, they might need to be quarantined longer. Koi have a recommended quarantine period of as long as 21 days.

You will be impatient, but this is a case in which waiting can prevent a wealth of problems and prolong the life of your fish. Also, this is the best way to maximize the return on your money.

It is important to make sure your fish will interact well with each other within the pond. Most pond fish will live together without issue, but if they eat the same things, you might have a hard time keeping them fed and healthy. Some more aggressive fish will target ornamental goldfish, such as shubunkins, and tear at their long fins. *More specific information about fancy goldfish is available in the next section.*

Popular Pond Fish

As breeders continue to play with the different kinds of fish that already exist, more different looks and breeds of fish are offered for sale. Those include the following:

Goldfish

Shubunkin goldfish.

Goldfish are the ideal pond fish for any situation. They add color and shine to any pond, are cheaper than almost any other fish, and are easy to care for. Almost any pond could use a handful of goldfish to provide background color. In ancient times, goldfish were thought to be good luck. For a first-time fish keeper, goldfish can be a lucky charm and bring them the confidence to purchase more fish. There are many different types of goldfish, varying from the plainest, most basic orange goldfish, to the more spectacular shubunkin. Simple, old-fashioned goldfish are so plain and simple you might have forgotten what they look like because fancy goldfish and more ornate cousins of the simple goldfish have taken over pet stores and ponds. Yet there is much to be said for old-fashioned goldfish. They get along well with almost all pond fish and will tolerate temperature variations. Goldfish are not overly susceptible to pond diseases because they can tolerate less-than-perfect water conditions. Comets and shubunkins are also goldfish, though with different colorations. Comets are red and white spotted goldfish with extra-long tails. Shubunkins have a different coloring altogether, more blue or gray than orange. Care and feeding guidelines for comets and shubunkins are the same as regular goldfish, which also makes them good for first-time pond keepers.

Then there are the fancy goldfish, the goldfish's pickier and more finicky cousin. Fancy goldfish sport spots, designs, and fancy tails, the results of careful breeding. They come in many varieties, their colors varying from black to white and back along the entire spectrum of orange. Some are bred to have large, bugged out eyes, or long, stylized fins. Others, such as the lionhead, have large, ornamental heads, meant to resemble the mane of a lion. Though they are more beautiful, the breeding also makes them weaker. Fancy goldfish are less hardy than their plainer counterparts. The fancy goldfish will require more care than the plain goldfish because they cannot sustain temperature changes and exposure to disease. Fancy goldfish will need to be removed from the pond as early as fall and placed back in a fish tank over the winter. They then cannot be placed back into the pond until the spring or summer when the temperature reaches 74 degrees consistently again. But beware because they do not like a water temperature any higher than about 3 degrees or 4 degrees higher than that, and they might require removal again if you live in a warm climate.

Though pretty, some gardeners feel fancy goldfish are more trouble than they are worth. There are tropical fish available that require transfer to a tank in the winter and are more attractive.

Tropical fish

Tropical fish are tempting to add to the pond because they will add eye-catching color and movement to the pond area. But tropical fish are meant for tropical temperatures, and they will need a certain minimum temperature in the water to survive. Not all ponds in all climates will meet their needs. A simple solution is to keep tropical fish in the pond for only a short while during the summer months, and place them back in an aquarium when the temperature dips below 50 degrees or so. This kind of repeated transfer every season is stressful for the fish and can be time consuming for you.

Koi fish

Koi are one of the most popular pond fish, perhaps due to their beautiful appearance. It is difficult to believe they are descendants of the ordinary brown carp. Genetic mutations brought out their color patches, and breeders attempt to create these mutations. Though they originated elsewhere, koi are associated with Japan because the

Assorted domestic koi. Photo courtesy of Drs. Foster and Smith Aquatics

Japanese have a special interest in koi and have years. The most beautiful and prized koi, bred by a reputable farm in Japan, can cost thousands of dollars. For gardeners just beginning with koi, there are relatively inexpensive koi available for purchase, perhaps online. They will be less reputable than the more expensive ones, but if you are not growing them to show, that should not matter as much. Investing money in your koi, if you know how to care for them, is a long-term investment because they will live in good conditions for anywhere from ten years on, as long as 30 years. If you purchase the koi online, make sure to check the store's policy before buying. Many stores that sell koi online think the fish becomes your property the minute they ship them out of the store to you. If the fish becomes sick during transport or after you get it, you cannot return it or ask for a refund. This might be the risk you take; just be aware of it before putting your money out.

Once you get them home, koi should be quarantined for as long as possible, from the standard two weeks to as long as six months. The breeder you purchase the koi from might recommend a longer quarantine period. Once you get them in the pond, after all that waiting, make sure they adapt well by making the pond to their requirements. Koi require a pond depth of at least 3 feet and like room to move around in, at least 20-25 square feet. Your pond should ideally be at least 1,000 gallons to accommodate koi. They like temperate water no hotter than 70 degrees. Koi are difficult and hard to please, but if you keep them happy, they will reward you with a sort of bond you will not get with any other fish. Koi will even learn to eat out of your hand and do tricks, such as jumping out of the pond. Many fish keepers find koi the most rewarding fish to keep.

Koi in popular culture

The beautiful koi is one of the best-known pond fish. Its image has become significant in other ways. In Japan, the koi holds a mythical appeal dating back many years. The koi is said to be a warrior of a fish, unafraid of man and sword. One popular legend tells how the koi swims upstream against the power of a waterfall and perseveres to his destination. It was the Japanese who first began keeping koi in ponds for display, long after the Chinese bred the fish as a source of food. They also began clubs, where breeders of koi could discuss the fish and compete against each other for the best-looking koi. The Japanese have distinct names for the different koi with their distinct color patterns. The most beautiful, high quality koi can sell for thousands of dollars.

In Western culture, the koi has become a popular tattoo. As tattoos have become more popular, the koi tattoo has become more mainstream. The wearer is expressing that they are someone of courage, unafraid of anything that stands in their way. The different colors of koi can represent different meanings, depending on the wearer's beliefs.

CASE STUDY: ADVICE FROM THE PET STORE

Gordon Magee
Internet Marketing and Media Manager

Ashly Hartmann
Fish/Pond Merchandising
Drs. Foster and Smith
P.O. Box 100 or
2253 Air Park Road
Rhinelander, WI 54501
www.DrsFosterSmith.com
www.FosterandSmithAquatics.com
www.LiveAquaria.com
www.PetEducation.com
715-361-9436
715-361-9465 (fax)

Drs. Foster and Smith sells more than 16,000 products and provides pet owners a one-stop shopping experience for dogs, cats, wild birds, caged birds, small pets, reptiles, ferrets, horses, and pet pharmacy needs. Additionally, Drs. Foster and Smith sells live fish and coral. It owns and maintains one of the largest aquaculture facilities in the United States in the frozen tundra of northern Wisconsin, from which it sells saltwater fish and propagates and sells saltwater coral. Its well-known educational website, **www.PetEducation.com** provides pet owners with more than 4,000 veterinarian-written or screened articles on good pet care, with subjects ranging from behavioral content to pet pharmaceutical and condition information. And fortunately for pond owners, they also carry a dazzling array of pond supplies, fish, and fish care products to keep your finned friends as healthy and happy as possible. Many Drs. Foster and Smith products can be seen throughout the pages of this book. For more information on pond supplies or fish care, visit **www.fosterandsmithaquatics.com**.

"From the beginning our mission has been to empower pet owners to take good care of their pets, by providing them with top quality, free information from the veterinary expertise of our owners who are of course veterinarians," says Gordon Magee. "Being a trusted source for pet care information has been key over the years. Additionally, our 100-percent satisfaction guarantee isn't just a marketing line, it is a reality at Drs. Foster and Smith. Over the years, people have come to know that we aren't just looking to make sales, but are looking to make customers — people with whom we have a long-standing and trusted relationship to provide them good information and fairly priced products. Knowing that we make good on that 100-percent satisfaction guaranteed promise has been a big part of making the company what it is today."

As far as its pond supplies are concerned, Drs. Foster and Smith only carries the best products for its customers and the natural habitats of the fish inhabiting their customers' ponds.

"We are excited about the technological advances in lighting with LED's and high-efficiency pumps," says Ashly Hartmann. "These products are better for the environment and bring down the operational costs for our customers."

As for which fish and water plants are most dear in the minds of the average customer, Drs. Foster and Smith gives the popularity prizes to koi fish and water lilies. Hartmann's favorite pond design she has seen so far among Drs. Foster and Smith's repertoire is "a terraced pond with multiple waterfalls that fits with the nature of the backyard. The pond can start at the top with waterfalls dropping into small pond and then more waterfalls dropping into a larger pond with koi fish and plants."

As far as new products to help the pond owner improve their pond environment for their fish, Drs. Foster and Smith recommends cleaning or updating the current pump and filtration system to make sure it is working to the best of its ability. "The biggest maintenance problems most pond owners run into are maintaining a healthy filtration system and clean pump," Hartmann says. "Ponds perform the best when maintaining maximum circulation."

And what advice does Drs. Foster and Smith have for the homeowner who is ready to add a new backyard pond to their home? "Research and educate yourself on the pond ecosystem process and fish," says Hartmann. "Plan what you would like and set the pond up this way from the start. It's difficult to go back and change the style of your pond" once you already have it set up.

Filters, Clarifiers, and Skimmers

A fish pond needs a pond filter. This will help the plants remove the fish waste from the water and balance the water's pH. Mechanical filters are fast-working units that trap uneaten fish food, fish waste, algae strings, or dead portions of plants. In so doing, they clean the pond and also keep this debris from getting caught in the pump. This is why most submersible pumps will come with a small filter attached. Because they do trap so much, this type of filter will require cleaning. Depending on the size of the pond and the season, this can be up to every other day.

Pondmaster 2000 Mechanical Filter. Photo courtesy of Drs. Foster and Smith Aquatics

Those who prefer a more organic approach can go with a biological filter. Biological filters convert fish waste to ammonia to nitrate. These filters hold gravel inside,

Fish Mate Pressurized UV Filter System. Combined biological, UV, and mechanical filtration system. Photo courtesy of Drs. Foster and Smith Aquatics.

which hold on to bacteria that can neutralize the fish waste. As an added bonus, biological filters will neutralize forms of algae. These types of filters require cleaning out on a monthly basis. The same as when you start a new pond, the biological filter will take time to accumulate bacteria. This is why it might take weeks for this filter to start affecting the pond's ecosystem. A pump needs to be used so the water moves through the biological filter at the right rate. If you are going to use a biological filter, you might choose to use an ultraviolet (UV) clarifier as well, which uses a UV bulb to zap algae and parasites. The clarifier will speed up the results the biological approach gives you. It will also counteract the tendency a biological filter has to promote algae growth in certain types of algae.

Lifegard Complete Pond Filter System. This system is perfect for shallow water ponds up to 3 feet deep. It features a fountainhead, UV clarifier, and mechanical and biological filtration. Photo courtesy of Drs. Foster and Smith Aquatics.

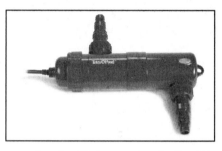

TetraPond® GreenFree UV Clarifier. This clarifier along with a good filtration system helps eliminate green water caused by free floating algae. Photo courtesy of Drs. Foster and Smith Aquatics.

Another piece of equipment that might not be necessary depending on your application is a pond skimmer. A skimmer is a different form of mechanical filter, one that traps dirt and debris inside a bag, which you

Savio Skimmerfilter. Photo courtesy of Drs. Foster and Smith Aquatics

can change out as needed. The frequency of bag changes can vary depending on the nature of your yard, but it is likely once a month in times of heavy debris, such as autumn, and less frequently at other times of the year.

Bottom drains

Pond fish waste needs to be removed or treated for the fish to continue living in the water. Overabundances of the elements they excrete will hurt them and possibly cause diseases. The food cycle begins when the fish digest the food. They produce ammonia as a byproduct of this process. Koi will excrete more waste than other pond fish, which is another reason they require more room than other pond fish.

In a pond specifically for fish, particularly koi fish, pond makers like a bottom drain, which will collect the fish waste and drain it from the pond area automatically. The drain is installed in the ground at a low point in the pond's bottom, and can be opened or closed to let water and waste flow out.

To keep the fish healthy, your pond has to meet certain requirements the fish have for their living conditions. Like children, fish like stability and routine. Fish will require a stable average temperature throughout the pond. That temperature will vary from fish to fish. Fish also like a certain pH, around 6 to 7, and they want that pH to stay the same. They need a certain amount of oxygen to survive. The waste they excrete will leave certain components in the water. These elements, nitrates, and ammonia have to be cleaned away from the pond, and only a small amount can remain.

Fish visitors

Your pond, now burbling away with water, perfumed with flowers, and chock full of fish, will attract more visitors than ever. Insects, small birds, frogs, reptiles, garden snakes, and raccoons might show up to investigate the area. These visitors will not be discouraged from visiting your pond and should not be. Some will serve a useful purpose in the pond area. Frogs and toads will eat the insects that gather around the pond, but, depending on the type of frog or toad, they can make croaking sounds that irritate your visitors. If turtles show up in your pond, they will likely eat your vegetation. Should a snake show up in the pond, the best idea is to leave it alone or call animal control to investigate. Even if you believe it to be harmless, it is better to err on the side of caution.

Human visitors

You will have many human visitors in the days, weeks, and months after your pond is completed and stocked, and though they will likely be excited and well meaning, they will commit some faux pas while visiting. Do not let visitors feed the fish or stick their hands in the water. It might be upsetting or stressful to the fish and might lead to overfeeding because it will be hard for you to keep track of how much food visitors have thrown into the pond area. Offer instead to let them come watch and participate in feedings at the times you specify. This way, they will feel included, and you will still be able to maintain control over your ecosystem. Also, make sure well-meaning visitors do not throw in a food item that is not meant for fish. Although some fish can eat small, protein-rich foods, such as shrimp, it is better not to have visitors throw any foreign foods or objects to them. Any item they do not eat will decompose and affect the water chemistry. Ensure also that if visitors throw food to bird visitors, they are not birds that will be encouraged to come back and prey on your fish. Also, make sure no trash gets left behind that might end up in the pond.

Testing the Pond Water

The water in your pond has to stay at a nice stable pH for your fish to stay healthy. To ensure the water is at this pH, test it regularly. Kits for testing the water quality of a pond are sold in garden supply stores and online. The kit will be straightforward and easy to use, containing test tubes, nitrates, ammonia, and instructions. There are also digital pH testers available, which look something like a digital thermometer. These are more expensive but can be used longer, so they might turn out to be a better value. You want your pond between a pH of 7 to 8, even 8.5. A pH too low will stress your fish, and they might have difficulty breathing due to the imbalance in the pond. The test also might give you the pond's nitrate and nitrate reading to further help you balance the pond.

Have a pond-warming party

Stocking your pond with fish can be a fun way to include the family and children. Include children in researching and picking the fish. Take them along to the store to pick out the fish. As it is best to only add a few fish to begin, each child can pick one of their own and release it into the pond. Small events such as this help the children to grow interested in the pond and feel included.

Be certain, though, that your children are old enough to handle it if the fish do not survive. Younger children might be upset if a predatory animal takes the fish, and this might lead to a longer talk about the predatory nature of animals. Be prepared to discuss it with them should the need arise.

Fish Food

Pond fish food is similar to aquarium fish food because it comes in flakes, pellets, or sticks. Some of the pellet food available is designed to sink, but exercise caution with these because much of the food might end up going to waste. Flakes are used to feed the smaller pond fish that cannot get at the pellets. Most pond fish will also enjoy live food, whether as part of a regular diet or as a supplemental

Foster and Smith Aquatics Staple Koi Food Pellets. Photo courtesy of Drs. Foster and Smith Aquatics

treat. You can try feeding your fish earthworms, bloodworms, or shrimp.

The amount of food and required feedings depend on the species of your fish, but there are guidelines to follow. In the springtime, your fish will want feeding because the plants and other sources of food within the pond will not be out yet. Because of the early point in the season, feed the fish light, easy-to-digest food. When they are more active, in the warmer time, they will require food with more protein. The fish food will likely

Blue Ridge Koi and Goldfish Staple Food. Photo courtesy of Drs. Foster and Smith Aquatics

have a suggested feeding schedule, which you can follow, but keep in mind these other guidelines:

- When they are at their most active, these fish should only be fed every other day.

- Do not overfeed the fish.

- Do not feed your fish in the winter. They are built to survive off the food they take in over the course of the year.

Fish Disease

Watch your pond fish for any signs of disease so you can begin treating them as soon as possible. There are a host of diseases fish can have, and curing them happens through different methods. Most can be helped through different techniques, such as a salt bath, but only cured through fish medication, antibiotics. As some fish medicines are harmful to plants, it is best to try and prevent fish disease where you can. Quarantine your fish before introducing them to the pond to avoid introducing diseases to the pond. Other fish diseases are not likely to be curable. With especially intense diseases, such as dropsy, you might even have to consider euthanizing a fish because it will become sick before dying.

Although each particular fish disease has different symptoms, keep in mind the following signs of fish disease; they are signs that a problem is present with your fish.

Symptoms of fish disease:

- **Changes in behavior:** You will get used to the typical behavior of your pond fish. After a while, you will know when to expect to see them swimming and when to see them being still. Changes in these behavior patterns are one of the easiest signs of disease to spot. Fish that you know are normally active, quick swimmers that suddenly become lethargic and huddle close to the walls of the pond might be experiencing the first signs of certain diseases. Fish that are responsive to you that no longer take any interest in you might also be sick.

- **Flashing or flicking:** Fish infested by a parasite might try to get the parasite off by flashing or flicking, flinging or scraping themselves against the side of your rocks. You might see the fish do this, or if they are fast swimmers, you might only see a quick flashing within the pond. Inspect these fish carefully, especially under the gill, to see if there is a swollen area. If not, there could be parasites present that are too small for you to see. Parasites also can be cured through fish medication.

- **Bloating:** Certain fish diseases will cause the fish to swell and bloat. They might swell in only one area, which can be indicative of a parasite. If they swell all over their bodies, this might be a sign of dropsy, also known as pinecone disease, because it causes the fish to swell up like a pinecone.

- **Visible markings:** Some serious fish diseases will leave a mark on the fish. You might see large sores, white fuzz, or white spots on the fish. These can be symptoms of an infection. By the time these signs appear, the fish is already sick. Even as you are treating this sick fish, think about protecting your other fish. Quarantine the fish that show these signs, and think about a treatment for the fish in the pond. A salt bath can be mixed into the pond if necessary. Follow the salt bath recipe listed below, but mix the salt directly into your pond.

- **Difficulty breathing:** You might see your fish reaching for the surface and making gasping faces as though they want to take in air. This difficulty in breathing is due to a high level of ammonia in the pond.

Infections

- **Fungal:** A fungal infection is acquired when the fish's immune system is compromised, in other words, when another problem is already present. The fungus will cause a sort of fuzz to appear on the fish. This white coating can be cleared up with fish medication, and you must try to determine if there is another disease affecting the same fish.

- **Dropsy:** An internal bacterial infection that is fatal to fish, dropsy, will cause your fish to bloat and swell. The fish's eyes might pop out of its head. The fish's scales will stick straight out and give it the appearance of a pine cone. Dropsy can be treated with antibiotic fish food and can be prevented by keeping cleaner pond water. But be warned that even with treatment, it is unlikely your fish will survive dropsy.

- **Ulcers:** A bacterial infection that causes open sores on the fish, which can be caused by stress or by a trauma. This is a difficult disease to eradicate from your fish, so the first step is to quarantine your fish as soon as you see an open sore. Consult a veterinarian for a recommended course of treatment, which will include a form of antibiotics.

Parasites

- **Flukes:** These parasites hook onto the fish and can be fatal if not treated. Your fish will be listless and slow moving or might flash and show signs of breathing difficulty. You can treat flukes with fish medication. A salt bath during the quarantine period might help restore the fish's health.

- **Whitespot/Ich:** Caused by a tiny parasite, a single-cell organism that can be normally present in just about any pond, the symptoms are white spots on the fish's body. It might look like a scattering of white dots on the fish's body. The fish will likely be listless and reluctant to eat. Whitespot is contagious, and once you notice the spots on one of your fish, it is likely you will see them on another. To prevent it, you can try maintaining a more stable water temperature.

- **Anchor Worm:** This parasite will latch on under a fish's gill and cause a swelling to the local area. The worms will need to be removed, and the fish treated with antibiotic. It is small and difficult to see, but if you do see it, you will see a long thin worm and an egg sac with two eggs in it. If you cannot bring yourself to remove the worm with tweezers, you can try subjecting your fish to an extra-strong salt bath to see if that drives the anchor worms away.

- **Lice:** Fish lice, which are incredibly difficult to see, can kill fish. The lice are clear and move around, which can make it difficult to confirm your suspicion if you are not sure what is wrong with your fish. Fish will bump against the sides of the pond to try and remove them. To treat them, remove them and treat the fish with antiseptic. Lice are likely coming in from birds that visit the pond, so be careful about encouraging avian visitors if pond lice are becoming a pest.

- **Microscopic Infections:** If your fish are flicking or flashing, one of these infections is a likely culprit. The parasites themselves are going to be too small to see, so look for a grayish slime emerging from your fish.

Salt bath recipe

Many diseased fish can be helped by a simple salt bath. This should be done before treating the fish with medication. You can mix 3 ounces of marine salt to each gallon of water in the quarantine tank or a spare tank. The alkaline of the salt will help neutralize the fish.

Family Activity: Stock Your Pond with Fish

Choosing fish for the pond can be overwhelming. The best way to make an informed choice is to research what fish suit your pond. Your children can help you decide which fish are best. Begin by taking a trip to the store where you plan to purchase your pond fish. As the children look around, have them make a note of the names and types of the fish that catch their fancy. Later, they can research the fish online or in your reference books to see if they will be able to survive in your pond, what special conditions and treatment they need, and how much room they will require. Depending on their ages, children might even be able to tackle the pond math involved in determining how many fish to stock.

Tropical or imported fish might catch the children's eyes because they are more bright or colorful. However, they will have a harder time surviving in a pond and will be more work for you in the long run. Domestic fish are able to cope with the temperature and natural plants in your area, while tropical fish might need your help every step of the way.

If you have a koi pond, choosing the fish becomes even more interesting. Help your children research about their distinctive colors, names, and patterns. If you purchase your koi from a Japanese farm, they can look at the location on the map and learn about it online. This knowledge can also lead to a bigger curiosity about Japan and other cultures.

Fish that spawn in abundance are easy to find for free, just the same ways that plentiful oxygenators can be found. A pond keeper's lore is that once comfortable enough to spawn once in your pond, goldfish will keep spawning, with increased output each year. Many overwhelmed pond keepers look to give away goldfish each season by offering them to other gardeners. Sharing the responsibility for the fish they choose can help teach your children responsibility. If they have been after you for a puppy or cat, this can be a good way to determine how responsible they are.

Watching the behavior of pond fish in their schools can be fascinating to children. The difference between schooling and non-schooling fish behavior can be noticeable even in a small pond. Children can observe the way your schooling fish move in a naturally coordinated pack, while other fish meander around alone.

CHAPTER 8

Light It Up

During the day, your pond will be a magnet for activity, drawing birds, insects, and the attention of your friends and visitors. At night, there is a different feeling to be enjoyed. There is a peaceful calm, a special kind of quiet. This is your time to sit, reflect, and enjoy the sound and look of the waterfall or fountain. Or, perhaps you have a large circle of friends and family who would be happy to come see the pond at night. Friday night can

Aquascape LED Bullet Spotlight.
Photo courtesy of Drs. Foster and Smith Aquatics

be unofficially held at your place as soon as the lighting is installed. For fish keepers, it also is a chance to visit with your fish alone and get a good unobstructed look at them. But how can you do that in the dark? You cannot. It is time to think about adding lights to the pond or the pond area.

If you have created a natural-style pond and envision this pond as a tribute to the beauty of nature, you might find it difficult to reconcile using lighting in this design. Lighting can be tastefully done so the viewer barely realizes it is there. This is a case where you might want to only use lights that can be hidden easily under other vegetation or within the pond water.

Lighting can be added to the area around the feature, the perimeter of the pond, or inside the pond. If you already have lighting around your backyard, the pond lighting will have to be styled in the same manner to allow it to blend in.

Creating a Lighting Plan

If you created a design plan for your pond, you might be able to use a clean copy of this to sketch out a lighting plan. If you need to do a smaller, more specific drawing of the direct pond area, it is worth it to have a clear idea of how your lighting is coming together.

More than a technical site plan and design plan, a lighting plan can be more conceptual and less detailed. The idea is to figure out how you will add the entire area around your pond. This might include the light you already get from existing sources, such as lights in other parts of the yard or on the exterior of the home.

Picturing the light

You want to find some way to assess and capture the amount of light that your area currently gets. But taking pictures to try to achieve this might not be helpful because the flash will defeat the purpose, and not using a flash might make the photo turn out too dark and worthless. A better idea might be to use a video camera, which could give you an idea of how much light is present.

How to Light Your Feature

The placement and angle of the lights you choose for your water feature will make a difference. Accent the parts of the feature you think viewers will want to see at night, such as the churning drop of a waterfall or the spitting geyser of a fountain. If you have created a viewing area, such as a table of a bench, consider how the view from the area will look at night. Consider lighting the area as the viewer sees it, with the light heading into the feature that way. If you do not have one special viewing area, consider the places people are most likely to stand or sit around your feature. A pond where there is no designated seating area might be a good candidate for lights around the perimeter. Consider small pathway lights, available at any garden store. Some of these lights are available in the solar-powered variety, which makes it easy to light the pond and stay green.

Pond lights should be made for this purpose because they will then be specially constructed for constant exposure to water. From LED bullet lights to large diameter halogen spotlights, different sizes and shapes are available to create any effect you might desire. Consider using multiple spotlights pointed toward the fountain or waterfall from different spots within the pond. This can be complemented with lights placed pond side or in the bushes around the pond. These types of lights, suitable for outdoor use, can be purchased at any large retailer or home improvement store.

If you still are leery of adding lights too close to the pond area, consider what around it you can light to illuminate the area. Other ways to create light around your pond:

- Place citronella tiki torches in the ground around the pond. Light them to get a soft glow on the pond.

- If there is a tree or group of trees nearby, consider how you can make it a source of light. Wrap the branches in tiny Christmas lights, or hang lanterns from the branches if they are sturdy.

- Add or increase the power of the existing lights on the outside of your home that point in the area of the feature.

Levels of light

When lighting your pond or your whole garden, it is important to consider the height of the area you are trying to light. In seating areas or areas where visitors will be milling around, consider the levels of light you have available. You might want to provide light at the following levels:

- **Ground:** Lighting the ground level is a good idea if you think the pond will be a party zone, where people will be jammed into a small space, where people are likely to be chatting and not looking where they are going, or where people will be intoxicated. You can use garden pathway lights to light the area or sunken lights placed in the ground. Consider whether the lights might be in the way of the same people you are trying to keep safe. Try to place them in places where they will illuminate the area but not in danger of being stepped on.

- **Conversation:** The conversation area is the area for people who are seated in your seating area or in chairs around the pond. This is more likely to be external lighting, placed on a table, or a light pole placed in the ground, or another form of lighting, such as tiki torches.

- **Pond:** Submersible lights, placed at the bottom or in the sides of the pond, or within the fountain spray, light the actual pond area. This lighting does not do anything to assist with lighting the viewing area or surrounding area, but it adds to the atmosphere and feeling. Depending on the effect you want, balance this light with the external light in the viewing area.

If you are creating show-stopping colors and effects within the pond, keep the lighting plain and low on the outside to retain the dramatic effect. Or if you are hoping to light the area outside more to encourage conversation and mingling, keep the light in the pond simple.

Getting equipped

Pond lights come with everything you need to install, so all you have to do is plug them in and place them in the necessary spots. A 120-volt system is the standard size used for outdoor electricity, though lower voltage systems are also available. These systems convert the current they receive from your home's power supply into a lower voltage. This is enough power to operate a small feature, yet not enough to electrocute anyone. To plug in your items, you will need a circuit breaker box and a power cable running from this box to your pond. You will need an outlet to plug these into, preferably a GFCI outlet. *More detailed information on choosing the supplies to install the electricity is discussed in Chapter 2.*

Types of Pond Lights

There are different lights that can be used separately or together to create the lighting as designed in the lighting plan:

- **Submersible** is the name given to those lights that go directly in the pond. These lights are made to stand up to being underwater and are, for all intents and purposes, waterproof. When placed inside the pond, it is difficult

Submersible Halogen Pond Light with four exchangeable colored lenses. Photo courtesy of Drs. Foster and Smith Aquatics

to see the light unit; the black housing blends right in with the color of the pond. Many submersible lights will change colors or effects as they cycle.

- **External** lights are ones that sit outside the feature, whether around the perimeter, at designated spots around the pond, or at a seating area you have created. To run either kind of light, you will need a power source for it. *See Chapter 2 for more information on what equipment is required for that task.*

Mini-rock lights. Photo courtesy of Drs. Foster and Smith Aquatics

- **Solar** is a kind of external light. Solar-powered garden lights can be placed in any area of your lighting plan that requires external lighting. They are available in any shape or design, even available in LED. Solar lights are a wise choice because they keep the electricity bill under control and are more ecologically friendly.

Solar Light Spheres. Photo courtesy of Drs. Foster and Smith Aquatics

- **Floating** lights, as their name implies, float on the top of the water. Many small garden lights, such as globe lights, are now equipped to float in water, adding a magical effect to the pond after dark. These lights might not be safe for ponds with fish in them. Even if they are safe from the manufacturer, if you have aggressive fish, you might choose to skip them.

Solar Chameleon Smart Globe. Photo courtesy of Drs. Foster and Smith Aquatics

When Do You Need an Electrician?

Some pond owners scrimp and save every cent they can on installation so they can call in a professional for other parts of the pond. It is true that using an electrician will require you to spend extra money and will take extra time. But if you are looking for a more complicated setup than the ones discussed here, it is the way to go. An electrician can make your pond dreams a reality. Want to have a switch on the wall inside your home from which you can have the power in the pond turn on and off? That is an electrician's job.

Want to create a light show spectacular that blinks along to music on a timer? That is likely a job for a professional.

If you want to use a professional but are worried about your budget, think creatively. One good way you can potentially save money is through referral. Ask friends, neighbors, co-workers, or the other professionals you have used through the course of this project to recommend a reputable electrician. Make it clear that you are not looking for an unlicensed friend or relative but rather a professional who might be willing to work with you a little on price. Many local businesses will have coupons in community newspapers or coupon books. If these do not get delivered to you, look for them at local small businesses, the grocery store, or online. Given the economic climate, people are willing to barter their work for yours. If you are capable of doing work that can be traded, do not be afraid to ask to barter services. You might not think the work you do is something with which to barter, but many services can be traded. Examples of work that can be bartered:

- Personal services, such as massage therapy, nails, or waxing
- Household help, such as child care, weekly housekeeping, or tailoring

- Home improvement services, such as yard work, cement work, or gardening

Ask your electrician up front what extra costs might be involved. You might have to pay for equipment, permits, and labor time for helpers. Also, get an estimate in writing that outlines what you talked about.

Safety and Equipment Minding

A word of safety: It is true that mixing electricity with water is dangerous; there is no denying it. However, given the knowledge the average hobbyist has and the quality of equipment available to us, it is safer than ever to experiment with electric-powered equipment. There are common sense actions that can be taken to prevent any accidents. Cover your external equipment from rain or splash-off water with a waterproof cover. There are covers for pumps that look like rocks or other items that camouflage it from view. Waterproof cord covers are available for any length of cord that is left exposed in your design. The act of adding lighting adds safety to the pond area because visitors will be less likely to trip, fall, or stumble over anything in the pond area once it is well lit.

In addition to being safe, many products make dressing up your pond simpler and more convenient. Wireless remotes use transmitters to allow you to turn the pond off and on at a button's touch, at a range of as long as 80 feet. This is much more affordable than having an electrician install a wall switch, and given that all you do is remove it from the box and plug it in, simpler.

Family Activity: Summer Pond Scavenger Hunt

Summertime in the pond can be a hotbed of activity, but if you cannot see in at night, you are missing half the fun. After installing lights under the surface or around the pond, you will be privy to even more pond activity than you are used to.

A fun activity on a warm evening can be a pond scavenger hunt, in which you and your children can search for certain items that are likely to appear. Schedule your scavenger hunt for a night that you are expecting one of your night-blooming lilies to open, and you will get a special bonus. Make a list of the likely visitors to your pond area based on the local wildlife. You can expect to see toads and frogs arriving after dusk to visit the water and nocturnal birds stopping in for a drink. Any recent hatchlings, such as little fish or tadpoles, will be fun to watch as they streak across the path of light. If you have seen evidence that raccoons visit your pond at night, be cautious and back away if they appear. Add a fun accessory, such as a color-changing solar powered globe, to add some fun to the night.

CHAPTER 9

Care and Maintenance

Now that your pond is completed, savor your accomplishment. To go from what might have been just a passing thought to a completed water feature takes planning and work. The time it took to map it out, dig it, and fill it, and the money that it took to get the right equipment, might have been difficult for you to come by. This is the moment your new feature begins to pay you back for this investment. If you have taken pictures or kept a journal to document the progress of your pond, you can now look back over them with satisfaction.

Do not forget to add pictures of the completed pond, so that 10 or 15 years down the line, you can look back with awe at how far your pond has come. If you have young children, you might want to pose them next to the pond, so you can look back at the growth of both. Enjoying time by the pond is the best way to start reaping the benefits of having a backyard water feature. But also take the time to care for your pond, so as to get the most value out of your equipment.

As time passes, you might want to add more to your pond area. You might find that you need to add things to help balance out the pond. Certain problems in your pond water will signal to you the need to add more plants, filtration, or oxygen. Although chemical treatments can solve problems in the short term, it is better to try to find a natural, long-term solution. Though chemical treatments sold for your pond are not harmful to your plants or fish, it should still be every pond keeper's hope to avoid them when possible. They can stress the plants and fish and will only buy you time, after which you are likely to be back where you started.

But other than this optional work, there is necessary work to be done. Once the initial setup of your pond is done, the most work-intensive part is over. Most of your time near the pond will be spent relaxing and enjoying the area. But even as you engage in pleasure time around the water feature, you will be engaging in pond maintenance. After all, if you see something in the pond area that is not right, will be you be able to relax until it fixed? Not likely. Nor can you help observing the condition of the pond, the water's color, and how well the equipment is working. Watching and paying attention is a large part of pond maintenance. Taking note of these observations will help you keep the pond healthy.

~~~~~~

Photo analysis

It might seem over the top at first, but taking a photo or two to document the condition and progress of the pond each week can pay off in the long run. When problems begin to present themselves, you can have an accurate idea of when the problem began and how severe it becomes. You can post these pictures to your favorite gardening sites online or take them with you to the pond store if you cannot figure out the source of your problem. In a garden pond, how quickly a problem progresses can be an important clue to its cause and solution. Set a day each week to snap a good shot, or do it when you can remember, but try to take them around the same time of the day. Try to get a good shot that shows the color and clarity of the water and the growth and progress of your plants.

~~~~~~

Care and maintenance of your pond will be simple tasks to help ensure the pond stays clean and free of debris. This will help the water quality of your pond to stay stable and in balance. A stable pond is a better place for fish and plants to live in because poor water quality can harm or even kill them. Certain water quality problems can even harm the liner and equipment in the pond. Others will ruin your good times by producing a strange color or a foul smell from the water. Care and maintenance will include easy things like cleaning the water's surface of debris with a net, up to more complex tasks like testing the pond water and analyzing the results. There is work that will be ongoing. To keep your pond healthy and in balance, you will need to do some routine care and maintenance tasks.

Your pond is a manmade addition to nature. It requires your help to survive because it cannot regulate itself. The system that naturally occurring ponds have for balancing the pond water does not exist in your pond. Also, your pond is stocked full of fish and plants, which need to be monitored to make sure they are playing the right roles in the pond and balancing the water. Many of these plants and fish are not native to your area. Their surroundings, from the soil to the water to the weather, are new to them. At this critical stage, you are the Mother Nature figure to your pond, which is like a new baby. If you do not assist the water in getting clean, it can become toxic to the fish. Invasive plants can get in and will take over and destroy the rest of the life in the pond if you do not find a way to remove them. If the pond becomes full of bacteria, they can kill the pond life and cause the water to change colors and emit a foul smell.

Pond care should take an hour or so of your time each week, perhaps two in the summertime. As you develop a routine and rhythm for these tasks, they can become part of your regular yard or gardening tasks. Most of these jobs can be anticipated and planned ahead, so they do not pile up and take more time. Keeping a schedule of the tasks and the frequency they need to be performed can help you stay on top of these and prevent costly problems in the future. Many of these tasks are simple, and older children can participate in them with you. After investing time and money in the pond, waterfall, or fountain, any pond owner would hate to be set back by trouble that can be avoided. Good short-term health can lead to a pond that stays healthy in the long run.

It might seem counterintuitive that a small pond would require more care than a larger one, but it is the case. A smaller pond, especially one stocked with fish, will get dirtier faster, so it will need more help from you to stay clean. If you have chosen not to use a filter in your pond setup, you can expect to have to do more work to keep the water clean. Plants will need to be added, and removed, if they are not helping to balance the water. In a filterless pond, the plants have the burden of keeping the water clean. This can be achieved but might require patience and experimenting. After the experience of a season without a filter, you might find you need to add one to keep your pond water balanced without too much intervention from you. Even if you have a mechanical filter, you might find you have to add a biological filter to balance the water.

Organizing Care and Maintenance

Keeping your pond in good health might seem like work, especially at first, when you are trying to get it established for the first time. Once you have more experience as a pond keeper, you will find the amount of work decreases. You will already know how to solve the problems that present themselves in the pond, so you will not have to experiment with different methods and waste time waiting to see if they work. Better yet, if you care for your pond well, the problems will go away over time. To get your pond to that stage, where it can mostly keep itself in balance, keep to a routine of care and maintenance.

Organizing your care and maintenance jobs by the frequency they need to be performed is one easy way to stay on top of them. Some tasks will have to be performed more regularly than others. Simple tasks, such as cleaning leaves and fallen branches from the surface of the pond, can be done on a daily basis and do not need a schedule. For the rest, you might find it hard to remember the precise time you last performed them. If you live in a temperate climate, how much your maintenance tasks need to be done will vary by season. If you live in an area where the temperature is more even year-round, you can expect to do the tasks as listed below:

Weekly maintenance

- Trim and remove any dead leaves on your plants before they have a chance to fall into the pond. You might need to do this more than once a week if your plants have taken off this year.

- Test the pond's ammonia level, along with the nitrite level. Take the appropriate steps to counteract any problems with these levels. If you are also going to monitor the pH level in your pond, you can administer this test once a week as well.

- Monitor the water level to make sure the pond is not leaking or losing too much water to wind or evaporation. Top up the pond with hose water or rainwater if necessary. Treat the water after refilling the pond.

- If any leaves fell into the pond and sank to the bottom before you were able to retrieve them, you might want to fish them out using a net with a long handle or a pond vacuum. Although some pond keepers do not go this far to keep the pond clear, others do not want the decaying of leaves to upset their pond chemistry.

Water Garden Outfitters Pond Vacuum XPV. Photo courtesy of Drs. Foster and Smith Aquatics

Monthly maintenance

- Clean your filter or pump. Make sure to remove debris from the intake screen and clean the individual components. If you have submersible equipment, pull it out of the pond and disconnect it from the power source before cleaning. Running submersible equipment when it is not underwater can be harmful to the equipment.

Seasonal Maintenance

The goal of your pond care and maintenance is to make it stable and harmonious and to balance it out. Each new season will bring different conditions that will upset the balance in your pond water. As the weather changes, there will also be elements that can harm your pond's structure and equipment. Keeping up with seasonal maintenance can mean the difference between replacing your equipment in five or ten years.

Some pond keepers live in those climates that change little year-round. If you are one of those lucky pond keepers, you will not have to make many adjustments to your maintenance schedule. In a tropical climate, however, you will find the pond needs maintenance because the heat will affect the water level and the plant growth. But this is a consistent schedule and will not need many seasonal modifications.

Pond owners in certain climates might have to anticipate extra work with the seasonal changes. In a more temperate area, the pond keeper will have to anticipate what each new season brings. Winter in cold climates can be hard on a pond unless that pond has been prepared for the coming cold weather. Similar, the high heat in other climates can wear on a pond.

If this is the first year for your pond, a large part of putting together a maintenance schedule will be through experience. There is much knowledge to be gained, and this is another way keeping a journal or record will benefit you. This first year will help you to learn what needs to be done and when. As the seasons change throughout the coming years, you can look back on your notes to help you remember what needs to be done at what point.

To begin preparing for seasonal changes, identify the zone you live in, according to the hardiness map in Chapter 6. The hardiness map will designate a zone to the area where you live, based on the average lowest temperature in your area. This will help you pinpoint how hot or cold it gets in your climate and what plants and animals can survive those temperatures.

Spring

In the springtime, your pond will be busy building itself up and getting ready for the active summer. If you live in a warm or tropical climate, most of your work in the springtime will be readying the pond for the coming season. The summer in a tropical garden pond is full of action. Spring is the time to build a sturdy foundation to handle the upcoming activity.

Stocking your pond with plants is a good first step. Divide and re-pot any of your existing plants that seem to have overgrown their current containers. Do not forget to trim your floating plants at the same time. With the increased sunshine in the summertime, you want your plants to be able to absorb some of it. If you have extra room, add any new plants you want to try in the coming season. Inquire and research whether the new additions can survive in the amount of room you have. Account for their anticipated growth through the summer. If you want to add new fish to your pond, spring might also be an optimal time to add them. Try to resist the temptation to overstock your pond. It would be a shame to waste time and money stocking the pond with new plants and animals only to have to get rid of them at the end of the summer.

Photo courtesy of Drs. Foster and Smith Aquatics

If you live in a more temperate climate, most of your work during this time will be replacing the items you removed before the winter. The pond will need to be re-stocked with its pump, filter, plants, and fish. If you have removed the pump, place it back in the pond before the fish go back in. This will give the pump time to get the water clean for the fish to return to the water. Your tropical plants can go in after. These will also help to ready the water for the fish to return to the pond. If you have decided to add a biological filter this year, spring is the time to begin so the bacteria will have ample time to colonize. In the case of a biological filter, it can take time for you to see any significant change brought on by this filter. The water will not instantly be in better condition, but over the long term, you will see an improvement. In the springtime, just like when you first filled the pond, there might be a large amount of algae in the pond. You do not need to do anything to counteract this because it is part of the pond's natural life cycles. The plants will help the problem once they start to bloom again and give out nutrients into the water. Some of the tasks you will need to perform in springtime include:

- Reconnect any equipment that was stored inside for winter, such as your pump and tubing. Test the equipment to make sure it is still working correctly. Make sure any pond lights still have working light bulbs and the electrical connections are still safe.

- Once the water reaches the right temperature, place tropical plants back in the pond. Monitor the air and water temperature carefully to be sure it is not too early to place them back in the pond.

- Fish can now be reintroduced into the pond. Monitor the chemical levels in the water carefully at this point. Any fish that were in the pond over the winter might seem sluggish at first until the warmer weather warms up the water and gets them moving. If you do notice your fish being sluggish and disoriented, keep a close eye on them. Watch your fish for any signs of trouble because the initial adjustment period will be difficult for them. They might be stressed from the move and readjustment to pond life. However, this is a time where they are more susceptible to disease, so be mindful of any signs of disease. Most pond fish will not need feeding until the water temperature rises above 50 degrees.

- Test your water quality to make sure the ammonia level stays low. If you find an increase in ammonia levels, check to make sure your pump is working properly.

No matter what zone you live in, spring is also a good time to do a check of your pond area to make sure everything is well placed and ready for another season. Do not forget to go over the following areas:

- Check the liner condition. Move edging around and look under it to make sure it has not damaged or ripped the liner because rips and strain on the liner, even in the area above the water level, can spread down the liner into the pond area.

- If you have built in plant shelves along the edges of your pond, make sure they are still level and have not eroded.

- Check all cords and electrical connections to make sure they are still working. If you have pets, check the cords to make sure your pets have not frayed or chewed on them. Wild animals, such as rabbits, can also be culprits when these cords appear to have been tampered with.

Summer

No matter what climate you live in, summer is likely to be your busiest time. Plants will stretch their leaves toward the sun's glow. Animals, from insects to birds, will flock to the water to socialize. Animal visitors will draw the eyes of your human visitors who will be drawn to the pond. Children will enjoy the drops that splash them from your fountain's spray and cool them off on the hottest afternoons.

Ponds that are home to plants or fish can be adversely affected by the raise in water temperature that comes with rising temperatures and extended sunlight hours. Sunlight can leech out oxygen, which is critical to the pond's health. Extra sunshine can also encourage ammonia to build up to excessive levels. All that sunshine can encourage algae to bloom. Even the increased humidity can have an effect. If you see signs that your pond's oxygen is low, a common idea is to add water from your garden hose. This water is not treated and will upset the chemical balance of the water, so you do not want to do this. You can run your pump to add oxygen to the water, or add

PondMaster Depp Water Air Pump Kit. This can be used to increase oxygen levels in large or deep ponds. Photo courtesy of Drs. Foster and Smith Aquatics

more submerged plants to provide a long-term solution. You might find yourself running the pump more than you have in the past, but this is normal in summertime, especially in a warm climate. It is also normal to have to top off the pond every week or two because it will lose water to evaporation and wind. Tasks to add to your list during the summer months:

- Treat or remove any extra buildup of algae. Blooms are normal and should not need treatment, depending on the life span of the pond.

- Make sure your floating plants are still balanced with the others. Thin floating plants if they crowd the surface of the water and block the sunlight from getting to the other plants. However, do not thin them out too much or you will risk a sudden bloom of algae. A good rule of thumb is that the floating plants should take up about 40 percent of the surface space.

- Monitor the insects around your pond. If they are harming your plants, rinse them off with a hose. Harmful insects include aphids, which you are likely to spot due to their black color.

- Clean any dead leaves or other debris from the pond's surface. If they sink to the bottom, you might want to fish them out. Decaying organic matter, such as leaves or fish food, can upset the balance of your pond.

- Wind or evaporation from heat can cause your pond level to lower. You might find you need to top off the pond with your hose once a week. If you find you have to do this, test the water to make sure it is balancing out. This new water will provide extra oxygen to your plants and fish, which they are apt to need this time of year.

- Check your fish because bacteria are at their height during this season. Be attentive to any new spots or discoloration on their bodies. Also, take note of their behavior if it has changed. Quarantining any sick fish promptly can save all your pond fish from being exposed.

- Take your pond's temperature. The pond will get hotter in the summer months, but it is important to keep the temperature stable because temperature changes can stress the fish and plants. It will also be difficult to maintain the oxygen level in your pond if it gets too hot.

Autumn

As the air grows crisp with the oncoming cold, the pond will become quieter and prepare for hibernation. Just as we associate the falling of leaves from the trees with this time of year, you can expect to see more of these leaves dotting the surface of your pond. One of your biggest challenges in the fall will be thinking of ways to keep these leaves out of your pond. If your pond only catches a few leaves, you might be able to fish them out by hand or with a net with no problem. It is important to the pond's chemistry that the leaves be removed. Some pond

keepers will even use a pond vacuum or long net to fish out leaves that sink to the bottom of the pond, rather than leave them to interfere with the pond chemistry.

After the rush of activity in the summer, your pond will begin to slow down as autumn progresses. You will see fewer animal visitors as they ready themselves for winter. Your maintenance tasks will decrease from summer to autumn, and you will find less clean up and care as the pond prepares itself for winter. Similar, take this time to plan how to prepare your pond for the upcoming colder months. At summer's end, it might seem that you have time until winter hits, but you might only have two months to winterize your pond. Your tropical plants will also have to come in before the first frost hits, which in some climates can be as early as October. If you live in a climate where the pond is likely to freeze completely, it is best to remove your equipment and fish. Check your pump for any parts that might need replacing at the start of the next season. Examine the tubing for any tears or parts that are damaged due to stress or rocks. Rinse your equipment and store it once it dries.

- Be vigilant about picking out leaves, branches, or pine needles that fall in the pond.

- If you have fish that will stay in the pond through the winter, switch their food to a more suitable food for autumn. *This is discussed in Chapter 7.*

- As you pull any plants out of the pond, check the roots for signs of disease. *Take note of any strange colors and refer to Chapter 6 on pond plants to see what they might indicate.*

Laguna Powerclean Cordless Pond Cleaner. Photo courtesy of Drs. Foster and Smith Aquatics

Winter

Even those who live in a tropical climate will see a decrease in activity in and around the pond in winter. The animal visitors to your pond will appear less, and though plants will survive, their colors will not show again until next spring. This can be one of the most peaceful and relaxing times for you as a pond keeper because the pond will require minimum maintenance but still be enjoyable, which is only one of the advantages of living in a warm place.

Those who live in more temperate zones will have to keep a close watch on the pond, even if it has to be done from indoors where it is warm. In winter, keep an eye on your pond to make sure that it does not freeze solid, especially if you have decided to leave some fish in there over the winter. If you have any doubt about whether it will freeze, err on the side of caution and bring your fish in. Letting the water freeze solid can damage or warp the pond liner and cause you to have to make costly repairs. It might mean death for your fish if they cannot breathe because ice will keep oxygen out. Fish will be alright, though, under a layer of ice, as long as the water is still moving under the ice, for a maximum of a few days. If your equipment, like the pump, is still installed, it can damage the equipment and cause it to break. To prevent the pond from freezing solid, there are methods you can try:

- Place several small balls on the surface, where they will float. The water around these balls will not have a chance to freeze because the ball will keep the water moving around it.

- You can also purchase a pond de-icer made especially for this purpose. The de-icer accomplishes the same purpose in a more high-tech way. It keeps a small piece of the pond from freezing.

- Get an air pump and air stone from a pet store. Used in aquariums, the air pump aerates the water by emitting bubbles through the air stone. The air stone will turn the water over enough to keep the surface from freezing. On especially cold days, make sure this equipment does not freeze.

Perfect Climate Deluxe Pond De-Icer. Perfect for small or large ponds and can be used as a floating or submersible de-icer. Photo courtesy of Drs. Foster and Smith Aquatics

- If your pond includes a waterfall, you can run the waterfall to keep the surface from freezing. However, you have to be careful that ice does not form and chip into the water flow. The pieces of ice can harm your equipment. You can remove any ice that looks poised to fall by hand.

Floating Pond De-Icer. Activates automatically once water temperature falls below 35° F. Photo courtesy of Drs. Foster and Smith Aquatics

- It is best to avoid melting the ice with hot water or breaking the ice open. This can hurt or upset the fish underneath or do damage to the liner. However, if you feel it is necessary to use these techniques, do it carefully and only to a small portion of the pond. If any damage is done to the fish or liner, it will only be to a small area.

When the water temperature gets to be lower than 40 degrees, stop feeding your fish. They will feed off the energy they have saved up all summer until spring hits and they start moving again.

Tropical plants should come in for the winter, but your hardy plants can stay. Pond keepers recommend sinking the plants in the bottom of the pond so they do not freeze. You can wear insulated garden gloves while working in the winter pond because the water will be cold. Specialty stores offer gloves that go all the way up to the elbow, to keep you from catching cold as you work outside.

Winter is the best time to plan for spring, If you want to make any changes to the look or styling of your pond, winter is the time to think about what new plants or fish to add. If you live in a colder climate, spend those winter evenings looking back over the past season and thinking about changes to implement.

Observing the Water Condition

Preventative maintenance is key to a healthy pond. Part of preventative maintenance is more technical — it requires you to test the water's quality and analyze the results. The other part is more old-fashioned; you must use your knowledge and instinct as a pond keeper. For example, after only weeks of watching the pond regularly, you will be able to tell if the water level in the pond has gone down. This can be the first sign of a leak, which can be patched up with an affordable repair kit or liner tape. If the leak is not visible, you can try pumping the water out of the pond to see if the leak then becomes visible. Or, the easier solution might be to drop food coloring into the water. This is not harmful to the fish and should create a stream of color directly toward the leak's source. Do not forget, what you think is a leak can be normal water loss due to other sources, such as evaporation or wind. It might also be a leak in the waterfall. If you have an attached waterfall, you can try turning it off for a few days and seeing if the water level drops. If the water level remains the same with the waterfall off, then the leak is likely within the waterfall. Take out the tubing that conducts water through the waterfall and see if there are any cracks or holes in it.

As your pond ages, you will see the water changing colors. After you first fill it, when the pond is full of tap water and plants have not had a chance to acclimatize, the water will be clear. As algae and bacteria start to grow, the water might turn a green or brown color. Although certain color tones signal a problem in the water's quality, brown or green water is closer to what you want than clear water. For example, a pond will be crowded with algae after it is first filled, which might give it a green tone. But at this stage of the pond's life, algae is normal. As the pond plants start to counteract the algae growth in the water, the pond will reach an optimal balance. As the plants perform their functions, the algae will slowly recede and the water will begin to look clearer.

One of the biggest hurdles in solving water quality problems is getting the right diagnosis. There are different problems that present the same symptoms. Observing the action at your pond can give you clues to solve future problems. If you build a pond, it will attract animal visitors. Though they might be welcome at your waterfront, they can bring uninvited visitors with them. Pond owners with fish should make note of any new animal visitors to the area because they might hold clues to future problems. Bacteria can travel with animals from a nearby water source to your pond, as can duckweed.

Checking the Water Quality

Unhealthy brown or green water is a symptom of a larger problem with your water's quality. Your pond is an ecosystem. This is no less true of ponds that do not house fish. All the elements of the pond still have to work together to create a healthy balance. Measuring the water quality is an important part of creating and maintaining that balance. Locating the imbalance in the water's quality can save you time by helping you to pinpoint a problem and its solution.

An imbalance of elements in the water can create larger problems. Those problems and their causes can include:

- A green pond is caused by algae. It can also be an invasive plant, such as duckweed, that has taken over the pond's surface.

- A brown pond indicates there is too much fish waste or dirt in the water.

An Introduction to Pond Chemistry

You might be wondering why it is necessary to test and analyze your water over again. Within your pond, there will be different elements: chemicals, minerals, bacteria, animals, and plants. Each must work together to achieve a healthy pond. Some of these elements will be toxic to your fish or plants. The elements in the pond can be traced back to one of two sources: nature or man.

Fish contribute to the water quality problems without meaning to. As the fish process their food, they will excrete waste into the water. The fish waste contains ammonia, which is toxic to the fish. In a small pond that is heavily stocked with fish, this ammonia can build up too quickly. You will need to test for these elements and take appropriate steps to combat them.

Chemical additions to the water

In areas where you are likely to fill the pond with tap water, it will pay off to find out from your water company exactly what is in the water. Chlorine can be traced back to the water you use to fill the pond. Tap water is treated with chlorine in most areas, which can be harmful to fish. Chlorine will naturally remove itself from the water with time, so you do not need to take action to remove it. If you leave it exposed to air for 24 hours, the chlorine will dissipate. Wait until there is little to no chlorine left in the water before stocking your fish. Plants can handle chlorine so they can be introduced to the water more quickly. Some areas will also treat the tap water with chloramine, which contains ammonia and chlorine. Chloramine is more of a risk to fish and will need to be treated to be removed. You can purchase chemical treatments, which will remove all the chlorine in the water at the same time and speed up the process. These treatments come as a liquid or powder you mix into the water.

Natural Additions to the Water

Ammonia, nitrates, nitrates, bacteria, and oxygen will each appear in a healthy pond. Even the toxic elements, such as ammonia, exist in the pond to serve a purpose. When the tested rate of ammonia is zero, that does not mean there is none present, which is a common misconception. It means the ammonia is converting into other elements at the same rate it is entering the pond.

If your pond is home to fish, you might be quick to point to them as the culprits when the level of ammonia in your pond is too high. Fish might contribute to the ammonia levels in your pond through their waste. But other sources contribute to the ammonia level as well, such as leaves or grass cuttings that have been allowed to drop into the pond. This is one of the reasons why it is important to take these items out of the pond when you see them.

The fish and their waste will also add two more elements to the pond chemistry: nitrates and nitrites. These are byproducts of the processing of ammonia within the pond water. Nitrates are not harmful and will help the pond plants to grow. They will, however, contribute to algae growth as well, so too many can be a bad thing. Though, because they are harmless, you do not have to worry about their presence. Nitrites, on the other hand, can harm your fish. *Information on combating nitrites is discussed later in this chapter.*

Bacteria is a welcome addition to your pond because it will help to break down the waste and other matter that is harmful to fish. You might see the bacteria as it colonizes on the rocks and flat surfaces in and around your pond, in a clear slimy coating. Even if this slime seems to be getting larger and thicker, it is not a cause of worry, because this is part of bacteria's natural life cycle. Bacteria do not require much to thrive, but they do demand oxygen. The appetite of hard-working bacteria for oxygen in the summer months can contribute to the lower levels of oxygen in the pond's water.

Oxygen is an element that belongs in both categories. Though the plants under the pond's surface will release naturally occurring oxygen, you can also add to the oxygen level by adding an aerating device, such as a waterfall. As a pond keeper, especially if you live in a warm climate, one of your main concerns will be the oxygen level and how to keep it stable. Many things in the pond, from fish to plants, consume oxygen, and in hot weather they will take it up as fast as it appears in the water.

Algae

Algae can be one of the most persistent pond problems. Algae will consume the pond's oxygen, deprive other plants of it, and leave them to die. They will spread to form a blanket across the surface of your pond and block the sunlight to other

plants. If left unchecked, algae can cut off the oxygen in the water to the point of killing your fish. There are different kinds of algae. The two that normally appear in garden ponds are single-cell organisms and filamentous or string algae. The single-cell algae is the kind that you see blooming in the pond after it is freshly filled. This is normal and will be handled by your submerged plants. Filamentous algae forms long, hairy-looking green strings. String algae can be hard to eliminate from your pond. The long strings can be hard to grasp and remove completely. This algae can also get caught, clog your filter or pump, and create more difficulty for keeping the water balanced. Removing it from your ponds is important because it will continue to grow and overtake the pond if left unchecked. If you can manage to remove it from the surface, this will also help to remove the nutrients that cause algae to appear. You can try to remove the algae with a stick or rake and dispose of it in your compost heap. You might not want to remove all the green you see because some algae is normal and even helpful to your pond. Algae that erupts on the pond liner or on the side of your rocks might be beneficial to the pond's ecology.

If physically removing the algae does not prove successful, you can try algicide to get rid of it. Using this method to eliminate algae from your pond, or get it down to a tolerable level, can be expensive and time consuming. Depending on the type of algae, you might have to purchase and try several treatments before one helps you to control the algae in your pond.

Algae thrive on sunlight to grow. One natural way to combat the algae is to leave less surface area open for sunshine to get through. Look at adding more plants that will take up surface space. Floating plants are ideal for this purpose, but depending on the type of floater, you run the risk of unleashing another problem. Floating plants can be aggressive, and you might find yourself having to thin them so they do not take over the pond. It is for you to decide whether this extra work is preferable to having an overpopulation of algae.

Certain pond animals will eat forms of algae, another way to control the problem naturally. Snails will clean away the algae that grows on your liner. These snails can be difficult to stock in a pond because pond fish will eat them. Wild snails might come to investigate your pond area but likely will not stay long. If you can get them to stay put in your pond, you will see your liner getting cleaner as they systematically inch along the surface. You can also get algae eating fish, similar to the ones you see cleaning fish tanks.

A Note on Well Water and Rainwater

Pond keepers who live in more rural areas might be able to fill their ponds entirely with well water. Test the water to be sure, but well water is ready to go and does not require any treatment before filling the pond and placing plants inside. Still, wait for the pond to stabilize before letting fish call it their home. This will give the plants time to begin working and be ready to counteract the sudden increase in ammonia levels that fish bring.

Ecologically minded people might collect rainwater in barrels to use when topping off their pond. This might or might not be preferable to tap water because rainwater is acidic and might need as much treatment as tap water.

As with well water, test the rainwater and see if it needs any intervention from you. Acidic water can corrode liner and edging if left that way for too long.

Testing the Pond

There are kits available to use to test the water quality in your pond. You can purchase them from a pond supply store. It is a good idea to keep some of these tests on hand in case a sudden problem occurs in your pond. Say you wake up one morning to dead fish with no animal culprit in sight. The fastest way to see if water quality is the culprit is to use one of the kits you have stored away to perform a quick test. You can then begin treating the problem.

Most tests are simple to use, and all you need to do is take a sample of the water in a small container and place a testing strip inside to measure the level of that particular element. The most useful ones include:

pH tests measure the acidity of your water's quality. You might remember pH strips from your high school science class. In school, you might have learned about the different pH levels and how they apply with your body. Here is a refresher: Inside your stomach, where food gets broken down, the pH level is normally very acidic, somewhere around a 2. Your mouth, which is less acidic, has a pH level of 7. To be a hospitable environment for your fish, your pond should also show a pH level around 7, although levels up to 8 are tolerable for fish. Either extreme will result in stress on the fish, who will likely exhibit behaviors, such as gasping for air at the pond's surface. An acidic pH in the pond will have a worse effect on the fish. In addition to gasping for air, the water might leech their color out of them and cause them to look even more sickly. To correct a pH level that is not healthy in your pond, try the following:

- If the pH level in your pond is unstable, try adding a buffer to balance it out. For example, you can add limestone under the water's surface or gravel on the bottom of the pond. These substances will help to balance the pH level in the pond. However, there can be additional problems associated with adding gravel or stones to your pond bottom. *More information on these can be found later in this chapter.*

- To combat a high pH level, try doing a partial water change. *More details on how to complete this is listed later in this chapter.*

- If the pond water needs to be more alkaline, you can try putting baking soda in the water to balance it. This is a foolproof treatment because too much baking soda will not harm the pond or fish.

Nitrite tests will help you determine if the waste level in your pond is too high. Nitrites appear in the pond as a byproduct of fish waste. Once the fish waste is secreted in the water, bacteria process it into nitrites. This byproduct can harm your fish and needs to be removed from the water. Any time you discover a level of more than zero nitrites, action should be taken. To combat the nitrites, try these steps:

- Do a partial water change of the water in your pond. Though it is not recommended to change more than about 10 percent of the water at once, to combat overly high nitrite levels, you might want to change up to 20 percent of the water. Do not forget to treat the water you add to the pond, if needed.

- To stop the nitrite level from getting any higher, minimize or stop feeding your fish. Once the pond water has been tested to show a nitrite level of zero, you can resume feeding the fish as normal. Do not worry about your fish because they will easily survive a few days without food and benefit from the lowered level of nitrites.

- Re-evaluate the number of fish in your pond. Though you might adore each fish, it might be best to remove some from the pond before they are all harmed. Alternately, look at what you can do to better clean the water. Perhaps it is time for a new or large filter. Depending on the type of filter you have, you might be able to place it on a higher setting to increase the cleaning power.

- If you are not using a filter, add one. Your pond water might need more bacteria to efficiently process the fish waste. The filter is the best place for bacteria to colonize and be dispersed in the pond water. If you already have a filter, make sure it is the right capacity for a pond your size. Examine the filter you are using to make sure it is not clogged and is working correctly.

Natural Ways to Balance your Pond

If your pond suffers from the same problem constantly and the cause is imbalance, the best tools for you come from nature. It is easier to come up with a long-term natural solution than to keep coming up with short-term solutions or use chemicals. In a natural pond, Mother Nature stocks everything and makes sure the ratio of each type of plant is perfect. As the pond keeper, you can try to emulate this to make the pond balance naturally.

If your pond needs more oxygen, you can add submerged plants to naturally aerate the water. These plants are not expensive, and in the case of those plants that grow particularly fast, you might be able to get them for free from a gardener who has an overabundance. Check with your local pond keeper friends, or look for people who give oxygenators away. Before adding these plants to your pond, know the reason they are being given away: they are growing fast in their current pond and the pond keeper cannot contain them. Inquire how much they are currently giving away and how much. If they are giving away bunches each week, you might have reason to be concerned about adding them to your pond. No two ponds are quite alike, so you do not have to assume things will go exactly the same in your backyard as they did in someone else's.

If you find your algae growth to be out of control, floating plants can help you minimize the conditions for them to grow in. Certain pond animals, such as snails, might help by eating away some of the algae. Koi have also been known to eat certain kinds of algae. Though their waste might cause problems, fish can also help you with a host of water quality problems. They can munch away on invasive plants, such as fairy moss.

Anacharis is a submerged plant that can help aerate the water. Photo courtesy of Drs. Foster and Smith Aquatics

If your problems are coming from fish waste, try the steps listed above. Also, consider adding a biological filter. This is a natural way of cleaning the water in your pond by using bacteria and other naturally occurring organisms. Barley straw is another natural aid to pond imbalance. Place barley straw in a permeable bag or a bag made of netting. You can also submerge a small bale of the straw in your water. As this is a natural remedy, it can take several weeks to see any improvement in water clarity. The barley straw does not take effect on the algae until it begins decaying. Then, it releases a chemical that is said to combat algae growth. This is still not a proven method, and though some pond keepers swear by it, others remain skeptical. Barley straw is a natural solution that cannot hurt the pond, so you can try it without fear. Those who do it change out the barley straw in the spring and again in the fall.

Adding a Biological Filter

Maybe you already have a mechanical filter and did not think you needed a biological filter as well. If you find that you are having recurrent water quality problems, now might be the time to add one. A biological filter takes more time to work than a mechanical filter but will help in neutralizing the toxins in your pond water. The filter acts as a home and breeding ground for bacteria that live on the plastic or rocks inside. This filter replicates what the natural organisms in your pond are already doing, but in a more concentrated space. It can take time for the bacteria to gather naturally, so you might want to give them a head start by purchasing bacteria to get the filter stocked and started. A good-quality filter will aerate the water before it passes through to the main filter, so look for one with an aeration chamber. This type of filter will need to run all the time for you to get the best results. Most biological filters are external units that sit in your yard not far from the pond area, but smaller submersible ones are available.

You will need to clean the biological filter occasionally. In the summer, you might find you need to do this more because dirt and leaves build up in the bottom of the biological filter unit. When cleaning the filter, be as careful as possible with the area where the bacteria colonizes. This can be any flat area within the filter but is foam, gravel, ceramic, or even plastic. Wash the filter enough so it does not clog or stink, but try not to scrub all the bacteria off as you do because that will defeat the purpose of having this filter. Do not use any soap or cleaning agent, and if possible, use treated water, because chemicals in tap water can harm the bacteria. If the bacteria get removed while cleaning, it can take another few months for them to build back up again.

Other Add-Ons

Other equipment can be purchased that might help you deal with water quality problems. These are not necessary to your pond's health but can be helpful if you have problems that just do not seem to want to go away. If your toughest battle has been with algae, a UV clarifier or sterilizer can help you zap the cells using an ultraviolet light that sits in the middle piece. This will also force the smaller organisms to clump together, which makes it easier for the filter to grab and remove them. The clarifier is stuck between the pump and the filter.

If the problem you have with your water quality stems from debris accumulating in the water, you can try adding a skimmer, which cleans debris, such as leaves and dirt, out of the water. This can be an ideal solution if you are constantly finding items stuck in the pump.

Home Remedies

When your children have a cough that will not go away, and the doctor's medicines are not helping, where can you turn? Old home remedies might be handed down from your grandmother or another person you know who is experienced that his or her word holds authority. Challenges in pond keeping might be better solved with homespun solutions. If you have friends who garden or have ponds, try to pick up tips from them. You can also look for these tips online.

Examples of alternative solutions:

- String algae is easily removed by wrapping it around a toilet brush.

- Plant vitamin stakes, intended for tomatoes, can be used to help grow any plants.

But, if your children still have that cough, you are not necessarily taking the advice of anyone online and going wild with it. Some of the advice and solutions offered to common pond problems will be controversial and even wrong. Use your judgment to decide which to try, and try them on a small section before expanding to the whole area.

Solving Common Pond Problems

To recap, the problems that plague garden ponds and possible solutions include:

- Foul smelling pond water: Though unusual colors are normal in the pond, unusual smells are not. Pond water that smells funny can be due to an overpopulation of bacteria. To solve this problem, the pond water

Duckweed.

will need to contain more oxygen. *You can aerate the pond in the ways specified earlier in this chapter.* In other cases, the smell is a symptom of a duckweed invasion. As the weeds spread across the pond's surface and overtake the other pond life, a rotting smell will also emerge. You can treat this by flushing out the duckweed, thereby also completing what is a partial water change. Begin by scraping as much of the duckweed off the surface of the pond as you can. Then, place a hose in the pond and raise the water level until the duckweed is lifted out of the pond. This will help to get the smaller particles of duckweed out of the pond. Dispose of the duckweed carefully. You might have to repeat this process several times to get rid of the duckweed completely.

- Oddly colored water: Green water can be a symptom of an overpopulation of algae. Whether to treat this algal bloom depends on where your pond is in its life cycle. If the pond is new or recently cleaned, this might be a normal bloom that will balance itself out naturally. If it is not a normal bloom, treat it with algicide as needed. But use algicide as sparingly as possible.

Rocks on the bottom

A debate rages between pond keepers who place rocks, stones, or gravel on the bottom of the pond and those who do not. Small rocks have been known to trap dirt and debris in them and make the pond dirtier. If you keep fish, their waste can get stuck under them and cause dirty, smelly water. After awhile, this type of waste will create toxins in the water. You might also see particles in your water that are visible to your eye if you pull a glass of pond water out and look at it in the light. However, other pond keepers use a pond vacuum to clean the pebbles on a regular basis and experience few problems. The same principle used in a biological filter is employed here in a larger scale. Rocks also will give bacteria a place to colonize and can be beneficial to the pond's health.

- Gasping Fish: Fish that are coming close to the water level and acting like they want you to feed them are hoping for oxygen. You can relieve the problem in the short term by adding hose water to the pond. In the long term, look at adding a pump or more oxygenating plants.

- Dying fish: Getting to the bottom of a dying fish epidemic requires some detective work. Take note of the kind of fish affected. If they were all the same kind, look at the breed specific diseases listed in the chapter on pond fish. If you had recently added a new fish without quarantining it first, it likely brought a disease into the pond with it. *See Chapter 7 for more specific information on fish diseases and how to combat them.*

Cleaning Your Pond

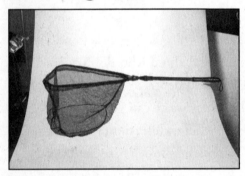

Laguna Soft Net. Features a telescopic handle and is tapered on the end to help collect debris and fish. Photo courtesy of Drs. Foster and Smith Aquatics

Although you might want to polish your water feature to a sparkle, it depends on what kind of feature you have. If you have a small, decorative water feature, such as a statuary without any wildlife, then cleaning your feature is fine. But if you have fish and plants stocked in your pond, resist as long as you can. Cleaning a wildlife pond will do more harm than good if you do it too much. Most ponds only need to be drained and cleaned every three to five years. Your pond needs bacteria to help it achieve a natural balance. If you clean the bacteria away, it will take the pond time to build them back up. During that time period, you might have to deal with water quality problems until the pond can naturally balance itself again. Your pond will be like a baby again, fighting off algae, pests, bacteria, and imbalance in the water. Done infrequently, though, a good cleaning will help the pond. For pond keepers with a chronic problem, cleaning the pond can be a potential solution, a fresh chance to avoid the problems you have.

There are circumstances that will call for the pond to be cleaned more. If your pond is situated in an area where the pond collects natural debris, such as fallen leaves you are not able to fish out, your pond might need some help staying clean. The same can go for ponds with a high concentration of fish.

When you are ready to clean the water feature, choosing the right time of year will make the job easier. It would seem to be a good idea to clean the pond in summer, when the plant and fish life is most active and can help rebalance the water. But trying to clean the pond in the middle of summer will prove to be more difficult than if you clean it in the later part of summer or early fall. This will be late enough so you can avoid the major wildlife activity, but early enough for the pond to re-generate some bacteria before the winter's freeze. It will also take away the elements that can harm the pond as it weathers the winter. Some pond keepers prefer to clean the pond in the early spring to get rid of the buildup accumulated in the winter.

Speed is a consideration when cleaning your pond. Taking the pond apart will take time to do. Putting everything back together will also take time. The actual cleaning should be done carefully, but as quickly as possible. The pond liner should not be exposed for any longer than is necessary because sunlight can cause extra wear and damage. Without water in the pond, any accidents that happen can be even more serious. Say you were to drop a rock into the emptied pond. This can rip or tear the liner, cause larger problems, and delay the cleaning process while you repair the tear and potential leak. Walking on the pond liner can also cause larger problems in the long run. If you have to walk on the liner, remove your shoes and tread as lightly as possible. Also make sure the equipment you will be using is not abrasive to the liner surface. If you choose a brush with which to scrub the liner, make sure it is soft and does not wear on the liner.

To preserve as much of the pond's ecology as you can, if you decide to clean your pond, everything has to be removed from the pond area. Only the liner should be washed, while rocks should be allowed to maintain as much bacteria as possible. Your plants and especially fish should not be exposed to the hose water you use to clean the pond.

How to clean the pond

Begin by pumping the water out of the pond. You can reserve this water in a tank or a children's wading pool to place the fish in as they wait to be replaced in the pond area. To accomplish this, it is best to remove your fish, plants, and any other small animals that live in the pond. You can then catch the fish as you drain the pond water. Depending on the kind of fish, it might be easiest to drain most of the water and then try to snag the fish. Smaller fish will be the hardest to grab, and you might choose to leave them for last. Before you clean the mud out of the bottom of the pond, remove small fish, frogs, tadpoles, lizards, or any other animals that will help the pond's balance as you put it back together. Any of these small creatures that you can preserve will help as you rebuild your pond. They will bring with them the beneficial bacteria that will take a longer time to build up naturally in the pond water. After you remove these creatures, you can use a plastic shovel or bucket to remove the dirt or muck remaining on the bottom of the pond.

Once everything is removed, you can scrub the liner's surface with a soft mop or brush. Make sure this cleaning tool does not hurt the surface. The fabric or bristle is non-abrasive and will not damage or tear your liner. You can use hose water to clean the pond, but it is not a good idea to use soap or chemicals. Instead, use a spray nozzle if needed to wash off any stubborn items that do not detach easily from the liner. Once you have the pond clean, you can pump the water that has collected out again.

Before you refill the pond, look over your liner. Search for any small rips or tears that you can repair or patch quickly. Note any areas where the liner is indented from edging or other items that press on it. You might want to move these items before the stress on the liner creates a tear.

Next, you can refill the pond with a hose. Treat the water as needed, and if you have saved any of the original pond water, you can add it to the pond. If you drained the pond due to a chronic problem, you might choose to start fresh with only new water. Once you have the pond refilled to the right level, place your plants back in the pond. The pond will need to recalibrate and reach a certain temperature and pH level before its inhabitants can be restocked into the water. Wait a few hours to reintroduce the fish until the water temperature in the pond is similar to the temperature of water in which they are being kept.

All together, this process can take all day, another reason to try and stick to partial water changes when possible, instead of scrubbing the pond area clean. Through the next few days or weeks, you can expect the normal problems associated with a newly filled pond. You might see a bloom of algae as the new water goes through a normal adjustment cycle. Treat them as you would if they appeared in your pond when it was newly dug and filled. Once your plants are back in the pond, they will begin to starve the algae into submission.

Partial Water Changes

Though you do not want to clean the pond more, partial water changes can be beneficial to your pond's health. Some pond keepers will conduct a partial water change once a week, with others changing the water only once a month. Changing the water will add oxygen and refresh the pond area. It will also help to keep the pond water clean. You can slowly filter out problems in the water through partial water changes without losing the beneficial bacteria the way you would if you cleaned the pond. Depending on the results of your water quality tests, you might need to adjust your schedule to do partial water changes.

Change about 10 percent of the water, up to about 20 percent in one partial water change. No more than that should be added to the pond without treating the water. If your tap water only contains chlorine, you can leave it out in buckets or containers for about a day and the chlorine will evaporate. Chloramine will not go away naturally and will need to be treated.

First, drain the amount of water you want to change from the pond. Then, add the new water. Do not forget to treat the water for chlorine or chloramine if needed.

An easier way to conduct the water change might be to use a pond vacuum. Vacuum out the dirt and silt in the bottom of the pond, and you might find enough water is sucked up with it to complete a partial water change easily. Then, add the water to top off the pond. Be cautious as you operate the vacuum because it can be easy to take out more water than you intended.

After conducting your first partial water change and seeing how your fish react to it, you might choose to do it more. Some pond keepers swear by frequent pond water changes to keep their water and fish aerated and happy.

Equipment Care

Caring properly for the equipment you purchase will help it last longer and work as well as possible. It will also save you from spending extra money that can be better used on other pond details. First and most important is regular cleaning of the equipment. This allows the equipment to work to its maximum potential. It will also keep regular buildup from forming large clogs inside the equipment.

If you experience a problem with your filter, take it apart and check to make sure nothing has clogged the pieces. If you have been experiencing trouble with algae, this might be your culprit. String algae, especially, can get caught up in the filter and stop it from working. Algae can also get stuck in the filter screen of your submersible pump. If the water in your feature is moving more slowly than usual, you might need to unplug your pump from its power source, pull the pump out of the water, and check it for clogs. Take apart the pump per the instructions that should be specified with the pump's manual. Clean the pieces individually to get it back to optimal power.

Your fountain spray will stay stronger if you clean the spray nozzle because dirt and minerals will build up over time and block portions of the spray. To clean the fountain, disassemble all the parts and clean each one individually.

Taking good care of your equipment will keep you from having to replace it needlessly. Inevitably, though, some equipment will need to be replaced over the life of the pond.

Routine Plant Care

Experienced gardeners might already have an idea of how much plants will need to be trimmed and re-potted. But the plants will act differently in the water. Some will flourish and grow faster, while others will grow at a slower, steadier rate. This is an important task but not one that can be precisely predicted until you get a feel for your pond and each of the plants inside.

Re-potting of plants is a task water gardeners perform seasonally as part of their spring preparations. Plants that have grown too rapidly can be divided with the remaining portion put in compost. If your plants grow especially fast, you might find you need to divide them again in the fall.

One person's trash...

If you do not have a compost heap and are reluctant to throw away these plants, you might be able to give them away. The old adage is truer in the garden world more than anywhere else: One gardener's trash is another gardener's treasure. Though your hornwort might grow to excess, another gardener might have difficulty getting oxygenators to take root in his or her pond. Ask around your neighborhood, garden groups, or online forums. If you still need to dispose of the plants, be cautious about how you do it, in case they are invasive in the wild.

To divide and repot your plants, you will need your garden tools, baskets, and access to your compost heap or buckets to temporarily store the plants you will be giving away. Begin by removing the plant from its current container. Inspect the roots for any signs of diseases. Cut back any dead roots. Divide the plant into sections for replanting. You can insert a fertilizer tablet into the soil as you repot the plant.

Mind your back

After time in the pond, the plant will weigh more than you recall. The water that has absorbed into the soil, combined with the weight of the plant's new root growth, will add to the plant's depth. Be careful as you bend to lift the plants that are submerged in the water out for trimming.

Taking a Vacation

Automatic feeders such as this can be installed to help maintain portion control and allow regular feedings when you are away on vacation. Photo courtesy of Drs. Foster and Smith Aquatics

If you are diligent about your regular pond care, you will not find much impact from skipping a task or two while you take a short vacation. Ponds that house fish, however, are a different story. Depending on the type of fish, you might be able to go a short time without feeding them. It might be a better idea to have a friend or neighbor stop by to feed them and check on them so any problems can be averted. Even if they do not have a pond of their own, they might be able to give you clues to the causes of problems that emerge after your return. The taste of pond tending might even cause your friends to contemplate creating ponds of their own.

Minimizing Your Maintenance

If you love your pond but find that the maintenance is becoming too demanding, there might be ways to cut back on the amount of care you need to perform.

- Nets: Placing a net above your pond might ruin the look you were hoping for. However, if your pond is placed under a tree or just seems to catch debris, hanging a net just above the water's surface can save you from having to constantly clean the surface of your pond. It can also save you from coming home to the debris and shock of your fish torn apart by predators.

- Renting Equipment: Some pond equipment might not be worth you investing your own money in but can be rented or borrowed. A pond vacuum can be useful to clean dirt accumulated on the bottom of the pond. It will take your pond water along with it, so you might need to top up the water level after using it.

- Containing Growth: Keeping as many plants as you can in containers will keep the dirt and buildup on the pond bottom to a minimum. This will keep you from having to vacuum or drain and clean the pond more than necessary. Floating plants should not be stocked in the pond in this way, but many of the other plants in your pond will thrive just as well inside the basket.

- Feed with caution: Only feed your pond fish as much as they need. In a true wildlife pond, most of your fish should not need feeding because they will be feeding naturally on plants, insects, and other small organisms. Any pellet or food flake left on the water's surface will sink and break down in the water. Just as with organic matter that gets in the water, leftover food will upset the water's chemistry. Follow the directions on the food, but if there is food left uneaten after about five minutes, cut back.

CHAPTER 10

~~~~~~~~~~

Happily Ever After

As long as your pond is being well cared for, you can expect a long life span out of the equipment and the pond itself. As the years go by, you will find yourself better able to predict the behaviors of your fish and plants, and pond keeping will become easier and more enjoyable. You might also notice patterns in the seasonal behavior of your pond. Anticipating your pond's seasonal needs will help you plan and reduce the time spent on these tasks. It will also help you enjoy the pond more once you know when to expect your blooms and animal visitors.

Changing the Look of Your Pond

When you first installed your pond, you were likely doing it to change or add something to your backyard landscape. A pond gives your yard a new energy. Excitement over the newly completed pond will drive you to spend more time in your backyard. The sounds of splashing water and pond animals singing will add to this energy. You will have friends and family come through the yard to admire your handiwork.

But as the years go by, the pond will become more like a member of the family. The backyard will shape around it, and caring for it might become tedious. After years of owning your pond, you might begin to get bored with it.

Photo courtesy of Drs. Foster and Smith Aquatics

Winter is a good time to think about changing the look of your pond. Once you add other elements to the backyard space, the style might change. Perhaps you purchased your home with several changes in mind that you did not get around to. As you make those changes, your backyard might take a more formal tone. Maybe the deck you hoped to someday build finally got finished. Even changes to the shrubbery or fence around your yard can inspire a change to the look.

There are small changes that can be made to your landscaping and pond area to change the look and feel. Swapping out the edging and plants for different ones can give a different view of the same pond and trick the viewer into thinking a major change was made. Changing the seating area and lights around the pond can also make the views look new again. New plants, lights, or edging can give the pond a brand new look.

If you are hoping to try out a new look this spring, consider one of the following:

- Adding new plants that grow to different heights than the existing ones will change the look of the pond. Consider also adding plants that grow horizontally, like ferns, because they will change the pond's shoreline. This will bring the eye down around the pond instead of up toward the surroundings and create a new focal point. If you hope to draw the eye upward, you can add tall grass, such as rush, or a small fruit tree around the area.

- Different lighting can change the look of the pond area. Adding submersible lights can make the area look more sophisticated and allow you to see more of the underwater activity happening in the pond. At the pond's side, try grouping lights into different configurations to create new focal points around the pond.

- Change the edging on one side of the pond to a pebble beach. To do this, you will need to create a slope on one side, if it does not already exist. Remove the edging on the side where you hope to place the beach. Roll the liner back to where the area for the beach can be dug without harming it. Then, dig a slope approaching the water on that side. Do not dig the slope too steep because birds and animals will want to get a foothold in the area. You can leave the dirt in place to create a lip before the water's surface. This should be a strip of about 1 inch thick, raised up to catch the stones before they can slide into the pond. Place your liner back over the beach area and cover it with the stones. If you prefer not to use the liner under this natural beach area, you can cut away the extra portion before covering it with the stones.

- Instead of adding things, try taking some away. Minimize edging and lighting, and return to a plainer look. Replace boulders or decorative stones with smaller, plainer stones. If your bigger problem is the time commitment and amount of work required with your pond, find ways to cut back on your responsibilities. To ease your pond fatigue, you can cut back on the amount of fish or plants in your pond, or take wildlife out. If you do not want to lose any of your pond creatures, you can add more equipment to help you minimize maintenance. If your pond is all natural, consider adding a filtration system to make maintenance easier.

- Perhaps the naturally styled pond you created to be the crown jewel of your backyard oasis is too wild and unruly looking for you. Or, maybe your perfect fountain set in a perfectly manicured lawn is too much upkeep, and you feel a pond that looks at home in an unruly natural setting would better suit your life style. Depending on how carefully styled your pond is, doing an about-face in styling can be easy or difficult.

Going from natural to formal

To change a natural-looking pond to a more formal one, a formal pond needs to be landscaped more than a natural one. As a result, the easiest way to begin switching your pond over is to landscape your water area from the natural look you have achieved to a more manicured, well-kept look.

If you have a plainer pond, consider adding a fountain, statuary, or waterfall. The easier option would be to add a fountain or statuary with a submersible pump. If you hope to add a statuary, be sure your pond can support the extra weight. Adding a waterfall might entail the extra work of digging a second pond nearby to achieve a two-pond setup. This will instantly give the pond a more formal look.

If you have more naturally occurring plants in the water area, consider switching some out for more expensive, less native plants. This will assist in making the area look less naturally occurring and more like a pond someone had planned and landscaped. Also, consider switching out your natural-looking edging, such as boulders and moss, for a fancier edging, such as polished stones or tiles. Adding more to the area will also help. If you have not already done so, consider adding a bench, lighting, or modern-styled railing to the area. If you already have these items, look critically at their styling to see how you can make them more formal-looking.

Maybe a wood bench can be stained with a different finish to give it a more polished look. A dark cherry finish, for example, looks more stylized than a plain oak bench. A railing made out of wood can be swapped out for one in a metal finish. If you do not have any external lighting in your pond area, think about adding some. The right lights, such as geometrical shapes trimmed in copper or another metal, can add a polished touch.

Going from formal to natural

Changing a formal pond to a natural look is easier than going the other way around. A natural pond requires less maintenance than a formal pond, so you can let yourself relax. Let your plants grow longer and stronger than you normally would. This will let the carefully styled edges of your pond to blur and soften.

Leafy, lush plants should be added to the pond margins to help with this natural look. Added plants can mask a more formal shape, such as a square or rectangle. Remove more formally styled items from the area. The aim of a natural pond is to look wild and unplanned, as though it was touched by Mother Nature's hand and not your own. Try to figure out the best ways to give the viewer this impression. If your pond is suitable for fish but does not have any living in it, consider adding some. They will give an added touch of nature and make the viewer feel he or she has come across a natural habitat for fish.

Expanding your pond

After years of adding fish and plants to your pond, you might find it too hard to cut back enough to accommodate its size. What if you cannot bear to give away any of your fish or plants? It might be time to take on an addition to the pond.

Photo courtesy of Drs. Foster and Smith Aquatics

If you built your original pond with a flexible liner, be able to seam this with the liner being placed in the new pond space. You will have to consider whether your old liner is worth hanging on to and seaming, or whether it is better to start over and dig a new pond. Reflect on the age and life expectancy of your liner when contemplating seaming it with a new liner. If half or more of the liner's life expectancy has passed, it is not worth seaming it with a brand new one. Adding to your pond will be difficult and can turn out badly if you do not seam the liners well. It might be wiser to create a new pond nearby and fill the area between them with plants, rocks, or a bog garden. If your yard is large enough, you can create a separate water area in another section of the yard with a different styling and feeling and stock it with plants and fish that overrun your current pond.

If you decide to add to your pond, plan the addition so the shape flows together. Take caution not to create any dead spots, or spots that do not circulate well, by adding the extension. When the planning is complete, the work can begin with digging and preparing the new pond site, the same way you did with the original pond. *For instructions on how to do this, see Chapter 3.*

Next, you will need to be able to access the edge of the liner in the current pond to create a seam with the liner of the new extension. If you need to, drain some of the water in your existing pond. If you have edging keeping the liner in place, remove these elements. Pull the liner up in the area where you intend to seam it with the new liner. This might require more than one set of hands because the liner will likely be slippery. Clean the section of liner you will paste to the new section. Any dirt that remains on it will keep the glue and tape from doing its job properly. Remove it as best as possible, but do not scrub the liner too hard or you will risk damaging it. You can then secure the two pieces of liner together using the adhesive of your choice. Pond supply stores offer kits for patching liner, or you can purchase glue that you paint on or double-sided tape.

You might want to coat it with a nontoxic sealant, such as silicone. Allow time for the seam to dry. When the liquids are dry, you can fill the addition and treat the water. Then, dig out the area under the joined liners to create a passageway for your fish. Use your shovel or spade to clear out the dirt under this portion. Then, add the rocks or edging back in to frame the new passageway.

Solving Your Existing Problems

Although you might not be working directly on the pond in the off-seasons, there is still important planning work for you to do. Winter is the best time for you to put on another hat: your detective hat. Mysterious problems might have plagued your pond over the past year or even several years. Perhaps you have gotten to the cause of the problem but have not found an effective, long-term solution for it. If you have kept a pond journal over the past seasons, you have all the clues you need to solve these mysteries. Look at the symptoms that appear repeatedly in your pond water, fish, and plants. If you have tried to solve these problems, take note of the solutions you have tried and what results they had. Tally up the amount of chemical treatments you have used. Minimizing this number is important because chemical treatments can be harmful to the water quality. Determine what plants can be added when you replant in the spring to try and counteract these problems. If you have been using the garden hose to aerate the pond throughout the year, not just in the summer when the heat is on, you might need to add more oxygenating plants under the water's surface. If any of the plants you added last year had problems adapting to pond life or even died, take time to determine if they should be repositioned within the pond or even moved to the pond's edge. Some plants will fare better planted directly in the moist soil of your bog area. Other plants might not have met your expectations and could be better off given to a friend who gardens or in your compost heap.

Similar, if you have fish in your pond, this is a good time to re-evaluate how many to place back in the pond in the spring. If the fish you have showed signs of overcrowding in the past season, this might be a reason to reduce the amount of new fish you add or not add any. If your fish spawned this year, have a look at your notes on how many so you can anticipate at least that many new additions in the coming year. Healthy fish need a clean pond with optimally balanced water. If your pond is overcrowded and the water quality suffers before you can recover it, some or all your fish can end up dying because of it.

Dealing with Mother Nature's Creatures

If you love your fish and hope to keep them safe from returning predators, plan to protect your fish from the creatures that will come to visit.

The added moisture and plant life around your pond will beckon to other animals who will want to visit the water's edge. Some of these animals, such as frogs, might help your pond's ecology and should be left alone. Other visitors, like snakes in southern states, might make you and your visitors uncomfortable, and you might need to have them removed from the area. Animal visitors you can expect to see are:

- **Birds:** Many pond owners find the opportunity to watch birds that flock to the pond an added bonus. Most of these birds will not harm your fish or plants and will add to your backyard's atmosphere with their

Great Blue Heron.

bright colors and happy songs. However, some types of birds will act as predators to your birds and fish. Herons can be fun to watch, with their backward-bending knees and silly-looking walk. But they have to be prevented from picking under the water's surface and snacking on your fish. Once a heron has the idea that he or she can snack at your pond, he or she will continue to return and you will have a harder time chasing him or her away. You might be able to deter a heron by stringing a net over the pond to protect the fish. If you do not like the look of a net, you can try stringing fishing line around the pond. Pond keepers have also tried scarecrows, motion detector sprayers, and loud noises to deter herons. Even a decoy heron might work for a period because herons are territorial and do not like to eat together. If you have ongoing problems with birds eating your fish, consider installing a shishi odoshi. *For instructions on how to create one of these, turn back to Chapter 4.*

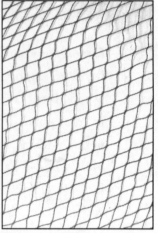

Laguna Pond Netting is used to protect the fish. Photos courtesy of Drs. Foster and Smith Aquatics

- **Frogs:** Frogs love an area where grass and water meet, so they can go back and forth. Your pond is a dream habitat for frogs, which also like to feast on insects in the vicinity. In this way, they will help you control the bug population in your pond area. Tadpoles will appear in the pond because frogs need to lay their eggs around the water. As they spawn, they will be entertaining for you and the children to watch. But they will also be beneficial because they will eat algae and mosquito larvae. Frogs are good for your pond. Do not try to stock them because that will create an overpopulation, but welcome them when they arrive.

Early Morning Singing

Frogs and toads are notoriously loud singers, and if they make a home beyond your bedroom window, you might be in for some sleepless nights. The croaking of frogs can be startlingly loud if you have not heard it at full force. There is not much that can be done about the sound. You can try to cover the noise with white noise, or perhaps music, but frogs are also famous for starting in the morning.

- **Toads:** Toads hold many of the same benefits for ponds as frogs do, although they behave differently. Toads live on land but will get in the water to lay eggs. Once you see a toad in the pond, it will not be there for long because they will run away to live in a land area. While they are around, though, they will help the pond area by cleaning it of bugs and pests.

Dogs, frogs, and toads

Think of the sunshine, the water's splash, and the buzz of insects. Your dog enjoys sitting by the pond as much as you do. Dogs will end up swiping at the animals in the pond and take one down on occasion. How to handle this practice is a matter for you to decide. But even if you do not mind your dog poking at the animals, do your best to ensure that frogs and toads are not on the menu. Eating a frog or toad or holding on to one can cause an allergic reaction in your dog. You might see your dog appear to foam at the mouth. The dog's mouth might also swell up, which can be dangerous. Most dogs will survive this easily, though you might want to rinse the dog's mouth with water. You know your dog best, so if he or she seems to be sick, take him or her to the vet just to be safe. Toads are likely to be poisonous, so be wary if your dog has ingested a toad.

- **Snails:** Like the other water critters, snails play a role in the pond's ecosystem. They will show up on their own eventually and come along with a larger animal or plant. You can purchase them at the pond supply store and stock them if you do not see any arriving naturally. Snails will help with pond problems simultaneously. They will eat algae and help clean your pond's water. They will also eat the debris that clouds the pond's water, such as decayed leaves. They can overpopulate your pond, though, and regular garden snails have also been known to carry diseases. For those reasons, some pond keepers loathe them. Most leave the snails alone because they benefit water quality, and if you have koi, the koi might eat the snails and keep their numbers in check.

- **Snakes:** In some zones, only harmless garter snakes can survive, and spotting a snake in your pond area is not a cause for panic. In other parts of the country, however, careful observation should be made from a safe distance until the type of snake is identified. Trying to prevent snakes from appearing in your pond is a fruitless task. In certain states, there could be a snake anywhere there is water, and not much can be done to stop snakes from appearing. The best thing to do is avoid them when you see them and call a professional to remove them if needed. Even if you are comfortable removing the snake and letting it go in another area, this is not recommended unless you have prior experience and know what kind of snake with which you are dealing.

- **Raccoons/Muskrat/ Possums:** In different regions throughout the country, you might have to deal with a sneaky, land-living, fish-loving predator. Of these, the raccoon is the most  difficult to deter. If you are already a gardener, you might have experience with this sneaky scavenger. Those who do not are surprised by the ferocity of raccoons. On first visit, they might just swipe your fish and scar others with their sharp teeth. But if the raccoon is particularity hungry, or if a family of raccoons come, do not be surprised to find your pond area leveled. Your potted plants can get kicked over and broken as they dive for your fish. They will dig up plants, tear apart edging, and even leave pieces of your missing fish behind. They are not picky eaters, and in addition to your fish, they will eat frogs, plants, and flowers. Swimming is not a problem for them, and they will get in to chase after your fish if necessary. There are ways to deter raccoons, with varying degrees of success. Though edging and shrubs or tall grasses around the pond might put them off, they are persistent and will try to find a way through. Because they are wily and flexible, they will find a way around sooner or later. In areas where the raccoons are persistent, pond keepers have resorted to alternate measures. For a smaller pond, a panel can be made of chicken wire, which you can lay across the pond to keep raccoons out. Those who would rather keep their view intact can try products that contain coyote urine, which is said to repel raccoons. In the wild, coyotes are a serious threat to raccoons, and the scent of their urine is said to be frightening. You can purchase the urine and sprinkle it in the area around your pond. In some yards, the raccoons and the pond keeper are engaged in a long-term battle. The raccoons return constantly, and the pond keeper nears desperation because the fish disappear as fast as he or she can stock them. If you are being plagued by raccoons like this and are ready to take more drastic action, you can build an electric fence around the pond. These electric fences can be purchased as a kit for this purpose from a garden supply store. You might be able to find those intended for dogs more cheaply priced at a pet supply store. You can also build you own using a 9- or 12-volt battery, wooden posts, and wiring. It might be best to have two wires, one high and one low, instead of just one, so that the raccoon cannot slide under or jump over. They have been known to outsmart the one-string setup. Because raccoons have become such a problem across the country, governments have gotten involved in their disposal. There might be local laws governing how to get rid of a raccoon, so check with the authorities to avoid a fine. Even moving the raccoon to another area is not permitted in some states. Because raccoons are territorial animals, some consider it inhumane to move a captured raccoon more than a certain distance away from where it was trapped. If this is the policy in the state where you live, you likely will not be able to get rid of the raccoon permanently, but you can find ways to keep them away from your fish. Opossum and muskrats have been reported to act in much the same way as raccoons. Though neither have the reputation for damage raccoons do, they have been known to destroy just as many fish.

Raccoons and Rabies

Raccoons are notorious as carriers of rabies. They are not the only animals with rabies. So why are they closely associated with the disease? Raccoons are known to make up a large percentage of the cases of rabies in wildlife each year. Across the country, from the southern states to Canada, even the raccoons in Manhattan's Central Park have been reported to have rabies. Many states attempt to vaccinate raccoons, through setting out bait that contains the vaccine wrapped inside some type of food or through a tag and release program. If you see a raccoon feeding at your pond during the day, it might be best to stay away. If you happen to be near one and it acts aggressively toward you, get away and call your local animal control office.

- **Turtles:** Turtles are docile and welcome visitors at the pond. But there are concerns that come with their visit. Turtles will eat your plants, including your beautiful lilies. They will shred leaves with their sharp teeth. Larger turtles can find their way into your pond and punch holes into the liner with their claws. But because they do not stay for long, the best thing might be to enjoy them while they visit.

CASE STUDY: CITY POND KEEPING

Pat Anderson
www.patanderson.net

At some point, you get humbled when dealing with raccoons and just sigh when they have uprooted another plant, drained the pond, or done something destructive, and just fix it, until the next time they do it and you fix it again. We used to board over our ponds at night. That is a maintenance headache and makes it hard to go out for the evening, even more difficult for the pet-sitters who have to come by and do that twice a day if you want to go away. We also tried using a water gun to scare the raccoons away. You have got to get them right on the tip of their nose for them to pay attention. However, it does not work well as a deterrent.

Unless it is nailed down, raccoons will move it. They are good at draining ponds. I have spoken with friends who have ponds, and they have found the same thing. It might be out of curiosity, but I think they do it because it is easier to grab fish when they are flopping about than it is from a full pond. We tried covering the ponds each night with plywood to keep the raccoons out and they managed to drain them down to the point that the pumps were sucking air (and burned out). If you are going to have fish, it has got to be a big enough pond with steep edges and hiding spots for the fish so the raccoons cannot get to them. And it should also be deep enough that it will not freeze all the way down (this can be helped with an immersion heater). Otherwise, the fish need to be brought indoors for winter.

I have a small garden pond and waterfall in my back garden. I had one in the front garden for years as well. My back garden water feature is made of a hard-shell kidney-shaped pond and a molded fiberglass waterfall with a small pump. When I had one in the front garden, it was rectangular and made from black flexible pond liner. I have planted an elderberry and Saskatoon berry in the back garden to provide some food. I like to attract birds because they need help — we have destroyed much of their environment. In Toronto, pesticides are no longer permitted for most uses, so birds can help with insect control. White noise helps to mask city noises, attracts wildlife, and enables growth of aquatic and marginal plants.

I get migratory birds in my backyard in the springtime. My backyard is a little city lot and only measures about 17-by-20 feet. Although seed eaters come for what is in the feeders, most birds come for the water. They can hear it, and they stop by for a drink or bath.

There is information out there. Read before starting.

Family Activity: Watch the Tadpoles Spawn

Children get curious about the circle of life at a young age. If yours are asking where babies come from, you might be able to show them if your pond is a place frogs or toads choose to deposit their eggs. If you want to see this, you can purchase eggs and stock your pond with them. Before deciding to do this, read on to be informed about the potential consequences.

If deposited naturally, toad or frog eggs will appear in the pond as small black eggs strung along in what look like spiderwebs around the edges of your pond. If you have fish in your pond, you might have to protect these eggs from them. Certain fish, such as koi, will eat the eggs before they have a chance to hatch. Other fish might just pull the eggs around, curious to see what this new arrival is. This can harm the eggs, so you might have to cover and protect them if you want them to hatch. Some types of fish are known to eat frog eggs, but not toad eggs, because they are said to be sour tasting. You can place the eggs gently in a basket or bucket in the pond, with water.

In addition to the fish, you might need to protect the eggs from being sucked into the equipment. Block the intake on your pump or skimmer with mesh. Check your filter and you might find them in there.

Depending on the number of eggs, you might choose to leave them be and let nature take its course because tadpoles allowed to hatch in the water might overwhelm the pond. If the eggs turn white, they will not hatch. You can remove them if they are easily accessible or leave them to decompose naturally.

Once the tadpoles hatch, they will be small, too small to emerge just yet. They will grow enough eventually to leave your pond and jump into the wild. Children may be sad to see them go, but they will have learned a wonderful science lesson first hand.

There is a possible drawback to this activity. The adorable and fascinating tadpoles might come back next year as lusty amphibians, eager to mate in your pond. For those who have not experienced mating season, prepare yourself for loud singing all hours of the day and night. The aggression that comes along with the lust can lead to you finding dead frogs or toads in your pond. Seeing dead toads after seeing the wonder of spawning might upset your children, and the number of tadpoles can be more than last year's. These tadpoles will gobble up valuable oxygen that your plants and fish need and upset the chemistry of your pond's water. After one year of dealing with frogs or toads returning to spawn, you might decide this is too much for you. If you do not want the tadpoles to hatch in your pond, you can relocate the eggs to a suitable wild area.

Shutting the Pond Down

Perhaps pond keeping has not turned out the way you had envisioned. Maybe the care and maintenance have come to be too much regular work for you. Or possibly the thrill of watching your pond develop has faded and you find it to be another chore you just do not have time for. However you come to this conclusion, do not take it lightly. Spend some time really thinking about getting rid of your pond. After all, you now know exactly how much work goes into creating a pond. Heaven forbid you should regret shutting it down and have to dig it all over again.

If you are considering eliminating your pond for good, consider the other ways of minimizing care as listed above. If you are sure you want to close down your pond, make arrangements to pass off your plants and fish to other pond keepers. Many of your fish can transition inside to act as household pets in a fish tank. Plants that cannot be given away can be disposed of in a compost heap. Do not dispose of your plants or animals in the wild, as they may be invasive and unsafe for disposal in nature.

Pull up your pond liner and fill the pond with dirt. If you have a pre-formed liner, you may have to dig around the outside of the liner to be able to pull it up. There may be dirt and silt in the bottom of the liner, which will make it hard for one person to lift and remove. If you are trying to complete this process on your own, you can shovel out the dirt and silt. Otherwise, call some helpers to assist in lifting the liner and dumping the dirt into the now empty hole.

You will need to re-fill the hole with dirt, and this large of an amount is unlikely to be easily pulled from another area of your yard. You may have to invest some money in purchasing the dirt, as having the open hole in your yard is not only dangerous, but can be a liability for insurance purposes.

Life as a Pond Keeper

If you already love gardening, adding a water aspect might seem like a given. After reading this guide, you can see how many choices there are. Building a backyard water feature is a decision to consider carefully. A fountain or waterfall can be nearly maintenance-free and ideal for those who do not have extra time. At the other end of the spectrum, a wildlife pond adds to your backyard's landscape but requires a long-term commitment. You are signing up for a learning experience, with new challenges each season and different problems to solve each year. Keeping a pond can also be more rewarding because your hard work will result in the pond growing and blooming each year.

Spreading the Love

As with any hobby, certain people are naturally suited to pond keeping. If you are one of those people, sharing your newfound pastime with others can bring a new level of enjoyment to you. In addition to the pride you take in your own garden and pond, you can take satisfaction in the ponds you have helped others create and maintain. Beyond sharing your love of pond keeping with your children in the ways outlined in this guide, you can share your knowledge and expertise in other ways:

- Sign up to act as a moderator or expert for your favorite garden website or forum. You can give advice, answer questions, and post pictures and stories about your pond. People from around the world use these sites, so this can keep you involved in ponding even in the wintertime in your climate.

- Give your excess plants or fish away to local gardeners. This will also help you to expand your network of local gardeners by introducing you to other pond keepers with similar tastes in fish and plants. You can also help others by giving some of your pond media, such as water or bacteria, to stock a friend's filter or pond.

- Once you feel you have reached expert level, you can sign up to teach classes at your local learning annex, community college, or community garden.

Life with your pond will be a challenge, but one that provides you beauty and satisfaction. Perhaps you choose to add a waterfall or a fountain. Either way, the enjoyment you derive from the area will grow to overshadow the effort. As the pond becomes part of your landscape and part of your family, you will wonder how you ever enjoyed your backyard without one.

Pond Plants

The following appendix lists the names of popular pond plants and a short description, including the scientific name of the plant, where the plant originated from, and the appearance of the plant. The zones of the U.S. hardiness map where the plants can survive are also listed.

When shopping for your plants, remember that certain plants can be called different names depending on the part of the country in which you are located. Breed variations might have a different name than listed but share the same traits with the plants described. If you are in doubt, check the plant's scientific name, which should tell you which plant with which you are dealing.

Certain plants are invasive in one climate and safe to grow as perennials in another. The gardening store or plant supplier may not have the most accurate or up-to-date information on which plans are banned, and some plant suppliers will continue to sell plants even though they have been banned. It is up to you to double check and make sure they are safe to grow and can be controlled in your zone. Traveling pond keepers might be tempted to buy plants they are not used to seeing in their home, but you can be fined for transporting invasive or banned plants into your state. Do not assume just because a plant is selling in a nearby state that it is allowed in your home state.

Anachris (anachris densa): An oxygenator native to South America. The majority of this plant is the stem, with small curled green leaves and the occasional white flower that appears above the surface. Although effective at aerating the water, this plant can also be aggressive.

Arrowhead (sagittaria latifolia): A marginal with small white flowers and rich green leaves. The stalks of this plant resemble arrows pointed into the sky, as the name suggests. Also known as duck potato, the plant can be eaten, and certain scavengers, notable muskrat, will come after it.

Anachris. Photo courtesy of Drs. Foster and Smith Aquatics.

Arrowhead, like lotus, is planted as a tuber, which can spread if planted directly in the soil of your bog.

Bog lily: The bog lily is sensitive to winter and can only stay out all winter in Zones 10 and 11.

Canna: Cannas can live in the water or in the bog soil. Terrestrial cannas, those that prefer soil, need to start out there before venturing into the water, or they will not survive. Let them grown to about 8 inches before you stick them under the surface. Aquatic cannas, the ones that like

the water, can go in the water and stay there, even in the winter. Cannas sprout flowers in colors reminiscent of the tropics, pretty pinks, and hot corals, but the color can range to deep reds and soft yellows.

Cattail (typha latifola): Often associated with the edges of natural ponds, cattail is a tall green grass with long, round brown tips. The roots of cattail can be sharp and should be contained under the water. Different types exist, distinguishable by the differently shaped seed heads.

Duckweed (lemma minor): A floating plant, which is a source of headaches and frustration for pond keepers across states and climates. Duckweed gets its name from the fact that it often travels to different ponds on the feet or bills of ducks. It can also spread from different plans in your pond quickly. A small green group of leaves that fish will eat, but might not be able to keep up with, duckweed is a plant that should not actively be added to your pond, and if it appears, you might have to skim it out repeatedly.

Fanwort (cabomba caroliniana): An oxygenator native to North America. Straight, long leaves like needles can grow underwater or above the suface. This plant can survive in Zones 6 through 11 but is banned as invasive in certain states.

Fern: Various types of ferns exist in different varieties. They enjoy life as marginals best but are known to thrive in divers conditions. Some ferns thrive in bog conditions. Ferns can also be considered invasive, as is the case with salvinia molesta, the Brazilian fern said to be one of the most invasive. Sold as a fish food, this fern has been banned in many states. The fern grows in

Photo courtesy of
Douglas Brown.

thick clusters that block sunlight, drain the water of oxygen, and inhibit the natural elements of the pond from working as they should.

Hornwort (ceratophyllum demersum): An oxygenator that prefers to be under the water's surface. This plant can survive in Zones 6 through 9.

Horsetail (*equisetum hymale*): A marginal plant, also called rush. These plants look like asparagus or bamboo, with joints or stripes of color coming to a point on a long stalk. They grow about 4 feet in optimal conditions, which is about any condition. They are known to be aggressive and are best kept in a container.

Iris: Irises can adapt well to either water or soil, so many pond keepers will place them on the edge of the pond. The flowers will burst open, with the petals arched away from the middle, as though they cannot get enough sunshine. The blooms are available in different colors, from yellow to violet, and every shade in between. Some types of irises are aggressive and have been banned in certain states.

Lotus: Fragrant and stunning, lotuses are worth every bit of work they require. Though most will only bloom for three days, they are still a beauty to observe the rest of the time. A lotus flower has long held a symbolic meaning and adds a touch of the exotic. In the wild, lotuses are native

to tropical climates, such as Australia and Southeast Asia. They can grow extremely large. The petals can extend 2 feet across.

Lotuses are purchased and planted as tubers. They are planted in a pot of soil and placed on the bottom of the pond, and the leaves float on the surface as they grow. In most climates, you will have to bring them inside during the winter. If you hope to keep the water lilies until next year, you might be in for work. People find this to be more work than it is worth and stock new ones every spring. Lotuses are considered a perennial, though, and they can sprout up every year in the right climates. Some breeds can survive through winter temperatures as low as -20 degrees. They will need two to three months of warm temperatures, at least 75 to 80 degrees, in order for the flower to bloom.

Some pond critters will try to eat your lotus plants, especially turtles. If there are turtles present in your pond, and your lotus looks like it has been cut up with scissors, they are the likely culprit.

If you are a late riser, you might miss the three days your lotus opens itself and stretches its petals toward the sun. The first day of bloom, the lotus will open from dawn until mid-morning. On the next day, it will open later, closer to 9 or 10 a.m., and stay open until about noon. Your last chance to see the bloom will happen even later, between noon and 3 p.m., on the third day. This is a good reason to plant more than one lotus if you have the space, just in case you miss one.

Lotus in popular culture

Like another pond dweller, the koi fish, the lotus has symbolic meanings in popular culture, as well as in tattoos. An ancient flower, the lotus is steeped in as much meaning as it is mystery. Across Asia, the lotus is seen to represent different things. The lotus also holds spiritual and religious connotations in cultures in the region. Buddhists and

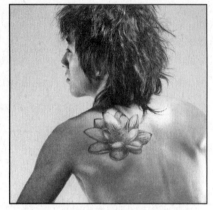

Hindus are two of the many religions that use the lotus to signify different things, from life's journey to virginity. Both religions have long shown their divine figures seated on lotuses, which are said to signify purity. In pictures, the Buddha sits smiling on a lotus throne, full of joy and wisdom. In Buddhism, the lotus is associated with the principle of remaining unattached in life. Popular names in Asian cultures can be translated to the word lotus or are derived from the word for lotus. Even in such diverse countries, such as India, Malaysia, and Vietnam, men and women have been named after this remarkable flower.

The meaning of the lotus tattoo is derived from the flower's traits. In nature, the lotus is said to start in the mud and rise to the top of the pond to become something beautiful. The lotus tattoo, therefore, symbolizes the journey of life or a variation of that idea. People will get it in memorial of a beautiful life cut short, while others want it to represent a difficult time in left that they have overcome. Again, as with koi fish tattoos, different colored lotuses can hold different meanings.

Many kinds of lotuses are available. Bright colors and large leaves are desirable in a lotus. Ask how large the leaves will grow, especially if you have a smaller pond. The floating leaves that accompany a lotus can grow to several feet long and overtake the surface space on the water.

American lotus (nelumbo lutea): A small lotus with white to yellow flowers.

Red lotus (nelumbo nucifera rosea): A lotus better suited to a larger pond, which will produce red flowers of a larger size.

Tulip lotus (shirokunshi): A small lotus with white flowers that imitate the shape of a tulip.

Milfoil (myriophyllum): An oxygenator that can be invasive in certain climates.

Mosquito fern (azolla caroliniana): A floating plant, called fairy moss, which can become an invasive pest. In warm summer heat, this fern can multiply to twice its existing size every week. It will require cutting back or thinning often but can be useful in a new pond, which needs surface cover from sunlight. If your pond is home to fish, they will likely help with the thinning because they like to eat the dark green fern. If you do not stock fish, think hard about adding this plant because the amount of work you have to do might prove to be too much and outweigh any cooling benefit it provides.

Primrose: A perennial that likes to live where the soil stays moist. Tennis balls of pretty flowers sprout around a tall green stem. The flowers on this plant can range from pink or red to purple or white, depending on the breed.

Taro (colocasia esculenta): A perennial, marginal plant native to Asia. Taro is grown as a root vegetable with large, floppy leaves. The plant is called elephant ears because of the look of the leaves. The plant can be cooked and eaten, but it contains toxins. The raw leaf will irritate your skin and should be handled carefully. Certain types of taro have deep purple or red colors woven into the green color on the leaves. Taro like moist soil and need a warmer climate. They can only survive in Zones 9 through 11.

Water hyacinth (eichhornia crassipes): A floating plant that produces a purple flower but is considered an invasive pest across the country. In southern states, it is best avoided, but it is safe in northern states, where winter will eliminate it from your pond even if you cannot.

Water hyssop (bacopa caroliniana): An oxygenator native to North America. Water hyssop can survive in Zones 8 through 10. Small green leaves form layers of half circles around fragrant purple flowers.

Water lettuce (pistia stratiotes): A floating plant that looks like the garden vegetable, hence its name. The different types of this plant can range in size, anywhere from 10 inches up to 20. This plant is invasive in warmer states but safe to grow in northern zones. Even in colder climates, remove as much of the plant as possible before winter hits. In addition to the invasive nature of the plant, it is a popular home for aphids. If you hope to add water lettuce to your pond, first be sure it is not banned in your state.

Water lilies: The large, distinctive leaves of the lily pad are a staple of backyard ponds: bright petals that, depending on the type of lily, might even change color. Certain lilies will stretch open toward the sun, while others wait for night to flash their petals. The colorful petals of the flower are beautiful and eye catching, but

Photo courtesy of Douglas Brown.

the lily pad also serves a purpose within the pond. It will protect fish from predators and protects against algae overpopulation by shading the water.

Although you might want to choose a lily based on the color of the flower, there are other details to consider. Ensure the lily you are buying is the right size for your pond. Depending on the type of lily, the pad can stretch to a large size. Certain breeds can stretch up to 10 feet.

Water lilies are classified into two types: tropical or hardy. Either type of lily will want sunlight. The water lily has to be potted and placed lower in the pond, even though the leaves will float on the surface.

- Hardy lilies, as the name suggests, are the less delicate lilies. They can survive in colder climates where it gets as cold as -20 degrees in the winter. If, however, the lily freezes down to the root, it is not likely to survive the winter. Hardy lilies come in beautiful colors, from pale pink to sunny yellow to pristine white.

- Tropical lilies need a warmer temperature to survive. They will need to be brought inside in the winter, unless the temperature stays above 40 degrees outside. They are known to be fuller and more fragrant than the hardy lilies, with more petals. Tropical lilies are more expensive and more work-intensive, so you might want to err on the side of caution and bring them inside even if your winters do not get that cold. Only certain tropical lilies bloom at night — they open up when the sun sets and close again as it rises.

Afterglow: Tropical lily with pink petals with touches of orange or yellow and a strong scent. The leaves will grow to spread 6 to 8 feet.

Arc en ciel (*rainbow*): A hardy lily named after the rainbow, this lily exhibits many shades and colors, from pink to red to yellow. The leaves will grow to spread 4 to 5 feet.

Chrysantha: The colors of a tropical lily in a hardy. It recalls an island summer sunset with shades of yellow with orange and pink highlights. The chrysantha grows to 2 to 3 feet.

Crystal white: Another hardy lily with beautiful white petals.

Dauben: A small-size tropical lily with light blue petals and a strong perfume.

Fabiola: A hardy lily in a warm red to pink color, said to be named after a Belgian princess. The fabiola grows to span 2 to 4 feet.

Firecrest: Pink flowers with a bright orange center. The firecrest is a hardy lily that grows to 6 to 12 feet.

Gladstone: A hardy lily with a larger size bloom with bright white petals. The gladstone reaches 5 to 8 feet.

Margaret mary: A vibrant blue to purple color petal. The margaret mary is a tropical lily that grows to 4 to 5 feet.

Missouri: A white flower with large petals. The missouri is a tropical lily that reaches 6 to 8 feet.

Pamela: Tropical lily in a soft purple color. The pameal grows to 6 feet.

Virginia: A hardy lily whose bloom points out at almost every angle like a star, with pointy petals in an off white to yellow color. The virginia reaches 5 to 6 feet.

Yellow dazzler: Tropical lily in a stunning shade of yellow, as the name suggests. The yellow dazzler grows 6 to 8 feet.

APPENDIX B

Pond Fish

Goldfish (carassius auratus auratus): Within the category of goldfish are the common goldfish as well as fancy goldfish varieties. These goldfish fall into the large classification of carp and are kin to the wild fish, as well as another pond dweller, the koi fish. Like the koi, goldfish can be traced back to China, where they were precious and valuable and seen as desirable based on the color they were. The Chinese bred goldfish to try to get lighter, golden colors instead of the orange hue we associate with them.

Anyone who has ever had a goldfish in a bowl or tank knows they are a sociable and playful fish. Goldfish like to have company and will not do well without goldfish friends inhabiting the same space. Pond keepers will introduce a handful at once because they have a harder time adapting to the pond than others and might not survive long. Their distinctive color will also make it harder to them to hide from predators, especially birds that like something with a metallic glint to it. Raccoons, herons, and opossum will all target your goldfish.

Common goldfish: Member of the carp family, along with koi. Native to Asia, goldfish are hardy and can live in different temperature ranges. Miniature breeds can be as small as 2 or 3 inches, while full-size goldfish can stretch up to 12 or 14 inches. Goldfish are famously easy to  care for and do not demand any care or environment requirements. They are a schooling fish and require company to feel at home in the pond.

Hundreds of fancy goldfish varieties exist, and breeders have created colors and distinctive traits.

Fancy goldfish: Bred to have distinctive appearance, fancy goldfish can be found to suit any look you like. Some have comically bugged eyes, while others have a Mohawk-style hump on their heads. The color of fancy goldfish can vary from solid tones of orange, red, blue, or yellow, to spotted or calico. Shubunkins are known for their long tails and spotted or varied color. They can range from a blue or black to traditional goldfish colors of orange or yellow. Comets are a smaller goldfish with a long, forked tail and a rounder body. Black moors are darkly colored with protruding eyes and calico-style white patches. Lionheads boast an impressive hump on their heads that gives the impression of a lion's mane. Fancy goldfish are harder to keep than common goldfish because they are not as hardy and need more stable conditions. After generations of being bred to produce certain mutations, fancy goldfish are known to get sicker and come with more problems. Some even have defects, like too-small bodies that crush their organs. They will not tolerate rapid temperature changes and should be taken out of the pond in the winter.

Koi (cyrprinus carpio): Member of the carp family, along with goldfish. Native to Asia, koi are an ornamental fish, sociable, and friendly. They like to live among other koi but have certain care requirements that are more involved than other fish breeds. Though koi can be more expensive than other fish, they can live for a long time and are considered valuable. Some koi keepers enter contests and clubs to see whose koi is the most beautiful and healthy.

Koi also have special requirements for feeding. Their main diet can be composed of the dry koi food sold in pet stores or pond stores. You may want to change the food with the seasons. Koi do better with a higher protein food in the summer and a lower protein food in the fall. They like other foods that can be given to them as treats, including worms, lettuce, and shrimp. They will supplement what you feed them by snacking on certain plants and rummaging in the muck on the bottom of the pond for things they like to eat.

Some popular koi breeds:

- **Butterfly:** A smaller koi that does not require as much room as the typical koi breed. The butterfly boasts beautiful fins on either side of the body. Though the butterfly is not seen as a true koi in the eyes of purists, they are well liked among pond keepers, who find them hardier and easier to keep than their larger cousins. Butterfly, like ghost koi, are the product of cross breeding between koi and carp.

Assorted butterfly koi. Photo courtesy of Drs. Foster and Smith Aquatics.

- **Ghost:** Ghost koi are another breed not seen in the eyes of purists as a true koi fish. This can be a benefit to pond keepers because they are not as expensive as other types of koi. The ghost is a product of cross breeding between koi and carp. They are characterized by a dark body with a shiny head and metallic fins that flash in the sunlight. These are known as good starter koi, a hardier, less needy way to ease yourself into the world of koi keeping. Ghost koi ask for little and grow quickly. Like the butterfly koi, they do not need as much room as other koi breeds.

- **Kohaku:** The kohaku is seen as the most popular type of koi, with its white body and spots in an orange/red color, like a cow. To identify a healthy kohaku, look for bright spots and strong white fins.

- **Shiro bekko:** A white fish with a black polka dot-style pattern down the back along the dorsal fin. The black spots should grow smaller along the length of the body.

Minnows: Minnow has become a general term, used over time to refer to different small fish between 3 and 6 inches. They like to travel in a school with more of their kind in the shallows of the ponds. Stock a handful at a time. Minnows can be particularly interesting for children to watch because they travel in formation around the pond.

Mosquito fish (*cambusia affinis*): A small dark fish, only 1 or 2 inches, that eats insects and their larvae. The fish is used to help control the mosquito population in an area where the insects are problems. They like to have the company of other mosquito fish and should be added to your pond in a group. In warmer climates, the fish can become a pest because they breed every two months and will overtake your pond. However, up north, the fish can be so in demand it is hard to find them for purchase. If you find they are overpopulating your pond, you can make a simple trap using a 2-liter soda bottle to try to rid your pond of them. They can survive some colder climates, so you cannot count on winter to rid your pond of them. Some larger fish will eat them, which might be the easiest and most effective solution.

Orfe (*leuciscus idus*): Another member of the carp family, the golden orfe resembles the koi and the goldfish. The orfe has an orange gold color, similar to a goldfish, with a long body similar to a koi. Blue orfe look more like oversize minnows, in a silvery blue color. A hardy fish, they will tolerate a range of temperatures and are not prone to illness. They grow from their initial size up to about 24 inches in the right conditions. One of the most interesting pond fish to watch, orfe swim rapidly and can beat just about any other fish in the water to food. They like to play around on the surface and will even jump out of the water to eat insects that hover over the surface. The fish mostly will stay in among the plants, though.

Sample Pond Design Courtesy of Drs. Foster and Smith Aquatics

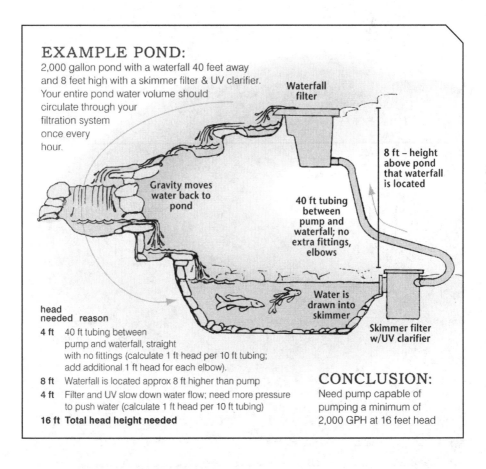

EXAMPLE POND:

2,000 gallon pond with a waterfall 40 feet away and 8 feet high with a skimmer filter & UV clarifier. Your entire pond water volume should circulate through your filtration system once every hour.

Waterfall filter

8 ft – height above pond that waterfall is located

Gravity moves water back to pond

40 ft tubing between pump and waterfall; no extra fittings, elbows

Water is drawn into skimmer

Skimmer filter w/UV clarifier

head needed reason

4 ft 40 ft tubing between pump and waterfall, straight with no fittings (calculate 1 ft head per 10 ft tubing; add additional 1 ft head for each elbow).

8 ft Waterfall is located approx 8 ft higher than pump

4 ft Filter and UV slow down water flow; need more pressure to push water (calculate 1 ft head per 10 ft tubing)

16 ft Total head height needed

CONCLUSION:

Need pump capable of pumping a minimum of 2,000 GPH at 16 feet head

Glossary

Algae: A single-cell organism, brown or green in color, that appears in bloom after the pond is initially filled.

Ammonia: A chemical byproduct of fish waste that should be treated if found in pond water because it can be deadly to fish.

Biological Filter: A filter that uses bacteria to balance and clean the pond water of harmful chemicals.

Chloramine: A chemical made of chlorine and ammonia that is found in tap water in certain areas. This substance is toxic to fish, and water has to be treated to remove the chloramine before fish can live in it.

Chlorine: A chemical introduced to tap water to make it potable. Chlorine will dissipate naturally after being left out for 24 hours, or the water can be treated to remove it.

Flexible Liner: A liner made of rubber, PVC, or EPDM, used to line the pond area and keep the pond water contained. This liner is placed on top of the underlayment once the pond is dug.

Mechanical Filter: A conventional filter that plugs in and cleans the water by trapping foreign particles inside.

Nitrate: A harmless byproduct of the breakdown of fish waste.

Nitrite: A harmful byproduct of the breakdown of fish waste. This compound is then broken down into nitrates.

Preformed Liner: An alternative to using flexible liner, a preformed liner is pre-molded into a specific shape.

Skimmer: A cleaning aid that traps large particles floating on the water's surface and removes them.

Statuary: A fountain where the water emerges from a statue and falls into a pond beneath it.

Submersible Pump: Any pump that circulates the water while it sits inside the body of water.

Underlayment: A fabric placed directly in the excavated pond site, used to cushion the area under a flexible liner.

Ultraviolet sterilizer: A cleaning device that shoots UV rays to eliminate waste particles and causes others to clump together, making them easier to remove.

Waterfall box: Used to collect water and drop it uniformly down a waterfall slope.

About the Author

Melissa Samaroo is a freelance writer who lives in Florida. She is also the author of *The Complete Dictionary of Insurance Terms Explained Simply.*

Index